SO-BJM-811

OBJECTLESSONS

A book series about the hidden lives of ordinary things.

Series Editors:

Ian Bogost and Christopher Schaberg

Advisory Board:

Sara Ahmed, Jane Bennett, Johanna Drucker, Raiford Guins, Graham Harman, renée hoogland, Pam Houston, Eileen Joy, Douglas Kahn, Daniel Miller, Esther Milne, Timothy Morton, Nigel Thrift, Kathleen Stewart, Rob Walker, Michele White.

In association with

LOYOLA UNIVERSITY NEW ORLEANS   **Georgia Tech** ‖ **Center for Media Studies**

BOOKS IN THE SERIES

glass

JOHN GARRISON

Bloomsbury Academic
An imprint of Bloomsbury Publishing Inc

B L O O M S B U R Y
NEW YORK • LONDON • OXFORD • NEW DELHI • SYDNEY

Bloomsbury Academic

An imprint of Bloomsbury Publishing Inc

1385 Broadway	50 Bedford Square
New York	London
NY 10018	WC1B 3DP
USA	UK

www.bloomsbury.com

**BLOOMSBURY and the Diana logo are trademarks of
Bloomsbury Publishing Plc**

First published 2015

Library of Congress Cataloging-in-Publication Data

Garrison, John S., 1970-
Glass / John Garrison.
pages cm. – (Object lessons)
Includes bibliographical references and index.
ISBN 978-1-62892-424-4 (pbk.: alk. paper) 1. Glass–Popular works.
2. Glassware–Psychological aspects–Popular works. 3. Glass in
literature–Popular works. I. Title.
TA450.G38 2015
620.1′44–dc23
2015011014

ISBN: PB: 978-1-6289-2424-4
ePub: 978-1-6289-2428-2
ePDF: 978-1-6289-2429-9

Series: Object Lessons

Typeset by Deanta Global Publishing Services, Chennai, India
Printed and bound in the United States of America

CONTENTS

PREFACE

In early 2014, a friend sent me a link to a short film by Corning. I recognized the company name and had a vague sense of it being a big manufacturer, maybe involved in making cookware. The film depicted an ultramodern household where every glass surface had interactive capability. I wasn't sure what to make of the film. It clearly resonated with people. It had over 24 million views on YouTube. As a longtime fan of science fiction, I was intrigued by the futuristic feel of the whole thing. Also, I used to work for a big consulting firm in the interactive technology sector, and our clients were mostly recognizable brands like Corning. A bit of online research told me that the company made much more than just cookware. In fact, it's a $10 billion company that has been a pioneer in all sorts of glass products, from light bulbs to windshields to iPhone screens. Having a better understanding of the company, I felt another connection to the film. My career started in the global strategies division of Levi Strauss & Co., another iconic brand with a long history—Levi's was founded in 1853, Corning was founded in 1851—and both companies have continually reinvented themselves to stay relevant. Of course, glass has been around for a lot longer than Corning. Thousands of years ago, the craft of glassmaking was being mastered in East Asia, Egypt, and Rome.[1] In Shakespeare's time, advances in glass technology were enabling new discoveries in science and new techniques in producing visual art. And here was another personal point of connection for me. After a first career in the interactive and marketing sectors, I moved on to study and teach Renaissance literature.

There's one more thing that struck me about the video. It underscored the very ubiquity of glass in our lives. Certainly, I already thought of glass as an object that one has around the house. We say, "Pass me a glass" when we want a vessel to fill with water, or "Where did I leave my glasses?" when we can't read the fine print. But glass is also the material from which so many objects (mirrors, windows, televisions, tables) are made. Beginning in the medieval period, the term "glass" was also used as a noun to denote a mirror, and beginning in the Renaissance, the word indicated an hourglass.[2] And just as glass is everywhere in the Corning film and in our homes, it's everywhere in Renaissance literature.[3] In my everyday life and in my scholarly life, it seems I am facing glass everywhere I turn.

What exactly is glass? Even my scientist friends gave me mixed answers. It continues to be debated whether glass is a liquid or a solid, as it stubbornly refuses to fall squarely into either category. Whenever I've touched glass, I've experienced it as being solid but, as this book will show, it has long operated in our imagination as if it has the properties of being porous, mutable, and evanescent. Glass seems marked by a profound instability, and not simply because the threat of it cracking or shattering is always imminent. It can be—sometimes simultaneously—reflective, opaque, or transparent. It can be used to gain perspicuity or to obfuscate, as well as to demarcate a surface while giving the illusion of depth.

Physical operations that we often associate with glass—gazing, mirroring, transparency—also function as abstract concepts to describe how we perceive the world and ourselves. Indeed, glass has long allowed writers and filmmakers to offer surprising, and sometimes counterintuitive, insights into the ways in which we choose to see the world and to see ourselves in the world. The recent emergence of interactive glass taps into our long-standing fantasies about the material as inherently responsive to our desire for connection. The more I thought about the Corning film and discussed it with friends, the more I began to draw evocative connections between the history of depictions of glass and emergent technologies that involved the material. For a long time, we've envisioned glass as holding unique promise for new forms of interaction between humans, as well as between humans and objects. Becoming more aware of glass called my attention to the very thing that is supposed to be transparent yet mitigates relations between people, information, and machines, as well as between people and their desired objects and experiences.

This book traces the connotations of one of our most familiar, everyday objects. Taking as its starting point new forms of interactive technology that turn walls, windshields, windows, countertops, eyeglasses, and other transparent glass surfaces into spaces of interaction and virtual experience, the book shows how these innovative glass objects transform the way we think about distinctions between surface and depth, transparency and reflection, solid and liquid. Examining a wide range of depictions from Shakespeare to contemporary science fiction film, I explore how our cultural imagination has long imbued glass with interactive capabilities that can generate new forms of intimacy and wish fulfillment only now being realized in emergent products and technologies.

The eighteen sections of this book, replicating the operations of glass itself, peruse, glance, dilate, and scan across a range of examples. Glass can do many things. Even when it's transparent and trying its best to be invisible, it's still affecting how we experience what is beyond it. And what it is doing to what we see is also what we're doing to ourselves when we look through glass. We, and glass, in any given moment might reflect, obfuscate, amplify, project, distort, or speculate.

"A Day Made of Glass"

Let's begin in the present, or at least a *speculative version of the present.* In its recent short film, Corning showcases its vision of a near future that takes us into a world where all glass surfaces offer ways to reformulate our everyday experiences. The title of the company's film, "A Day Made of Glass," imbues the material with worldmaking capabilities. We'll see this formulation echoed throughout this book, ranging from a sixteenth-century epic poem by Edmund Spenser that depicts "a world of glass" to the marketing site for Google Glass that exclaims, "Welcome to a world through Glass." In its film, Corning sees our days and worlds populated by bathroom mirrors, home windows, and car windshields ready to customize our present-moment experiences and offer us immediate access to the future experiences.

The video begins at "7:00 a.m. In The Near Future." We're in a bedroom, where a woman and a man are waking up. The house embodies a familiar vision of the future as if to be comforting to us, embracing the appearance of modern or ultramodern design. The house is uncluttered, marked by clean lines. A glass panel on the wall wakes the couple with birdsong; subsequently the photovoltaic floor-to-ceiling window shifts from opaque to transparent, bathing the room in sunlight—no need for drapes or shutters. The furniture, cabinets, and floors are beige and other natural colors. Corning's future is an idealized form of the present.

FIGURE 1 Interactive bathroom mirror (Still from "A Day Made of Glass"; image provided by Corning Incorporated).

However, the video isn't just *set in the future*. Importantly, it's about how glass *enables access to the future*. The woman's day commences with brushing her teeth and looking at herself in a mirror built from architectural display glass. While doing so, she accesses a calendar within the mirror to see what her day will bring.

There is no separate computer screen; the interface is built into the glass without frames or partitions to separate her from how her day will play out. The mirror summons the very near future of the day into the mind. The mirror reflects back the present moment of teeth brushing in crystal clarity while also projecting the future moment in the form of a calendar. The promise of glass is the promise of seamless simultaneity.

In the kitchen, photos and video are built into the veneer-glass surface of the refrigerator; no more snapshots or clunky magnets. Still photos come to life as video in the presence of

FIGURE 2 Interactive kitchen counter (Still from "A Day Made of Glass"; image provided by Corning Incorporated).

the waking family; no need to reach for a smart phone to see a photo or a snippet of video. The daughter draws whiskers and eyeglasses on one of the faces in an image on the fridge. In both the shift from still to video and the doodling, a past moment is made no longer static, is revivified through movement and altered to reflect the playful mood of the morning. Architectural surface glass, thermally durable and display enabling, simulates the appearance of old-style stove burner coils as it heats a pan. The same surface projects the future with the weather outlook.

The glass surface keeps the mind always in the future, just as a map on a clear surface in the car will plot a route to the family's destination—a functionality we see reoccurring in a glass bus shelter shortly after the scene in the kitchen.

Before the family leaves the house, though, a call comes in on the phone (a simple, rectangular piece of handheld display glass). The video call is transferred to the kitchen counter by touching the surface of the phone to it. Soon, dad and daughters are all speaking to grandma on the kitchen counter. The film reiterates several times that we're seeing "immersive, frameless glass." This phrase operates as both a technical description of the display format and a message about how seamlessly these objects will offer deeper engagement with our everyday world by fitting effortlessly into it. We're reminded here that glass enables connection between people, between multiple people. Indeed, all the interactive glass we see in the film is multi-touch (i.e., multiple users can manipulate the screen at once) and is often used for communication or collaboration with users in other locations. This is not the cold, techno-dominated future world we've been warned about, where glass screens make us more and more isolated.

In one of these scenes of collaboration, a small square of glass (like the phone we saw earlier) is placed on a glass table, bringing the surface to life with design details for clothing and a video of models wearing these clothes. The table, like all the glass surfaces we see in the film, is touch-sensitive. This choreographed move—where a small object holding data is placed on a glass table that brings that data to life—is one that we'll see later in examples ranging from automaker Scion's sales strategies to speculative technologies in *The Amazing Spider-Man 2*. When glass tables interface with other glass objects, there is no further need for a separate computer screen as everything can serve as a screen. In addition to the company that designs clothes, other retailers are featured in the film. The film does not just *sell* the idea of interactive glass to consumers; it emphasizes to the business sector that glass sells *products*. Glass enables us to imagine future, more appealing iterations of products and then to showcase those objects for individuals who might desire them.

Corning made a second short film, released a year later in 2012, entitled "A Day Made of Glass 2: Same Day." It is the same world, the same family. This time, the narrative opens with a scene from one of the children's perspective. Music from a handheld display-glass tablet wakes the girl. Three-dimensional, holographic images project from her tablet. The first ones are the sun and images of her with friends. It's as if the jumbled visuals from her dreams wake her to consciousness. The holograms then become more recognizable. We see the weather forecast and a quick text message demanding reply. Like her mother's bathroom mirror, the daughter's closet door is comprised of display glass with frameless information displays about the future: the week's weather forecast, reminders about what to bring to school, notice of a field trip to Redwood State Park that day. Tapping the word "Clothing" in the closet door, she is able to plan her outfit in the virtual space of the mirror before grabbing clothes from the closet.

The scene is a reminder of the peculiar dynamics of looking in the mirror. We often think we look at our reflection to answer the question, "How do I look?" However, the real question is "How will I look when others look at me?" Corning's scene makes such motivation

FIGURE 3 Choosing shoes for a day hike (Still from "A Day Made of Glass 2: Same Day"; image provided by Corning Incorporated).

explicit by blending the examination of one's reflection with a projection into the near future as the daughter plans how she will look for the day.

In the car, the daughter and her sister set the glass dashboard to display hearts as a surprise for their father, who laughs and also sees a reminder that he has a meeting a little over an hour away. Glass keeps us in the present by always reminding us about the future. After dropping the girls off at school, the father follows information on large-format display glass, which replaces freeway signs, that alerts him to construction or accidents. As a montage of scenes show us even more applications of glass in this world, there's one scene worth mentioning at this point. A doctor, who seems to be in a hospital in the United States, looks at a display of information on wall-format display glass. He's reading about a patient who is being treated by a doctor who appears to be in Asia. Soon, both doctors are looking at the same wall display simultaneously, but the wall is transparent. So, they are able to see each other and speak face-to-face through a glass wall as if inches away from each other. It's one more reminder that the day made of glass is anything but isolating.

Corning's effort to show us the possible ubiquity of glass in our near future underscores the linkage between glass and the stuff of fantasy. The film and the material it spotlights bring new worlds into focus. Glass, as an interactive material, embeds future experiences into present ones and promises new forms of relationality.

Macbeth

In order to better understand our present-day association between glass and the future, let us turn to a particularly curious moment in Shakespeare's *The Tragedy of Macbeth* (c. 1606). Macbeth confronts the witches and demands to know

> if your art
> Can tell so much: shall Banquo's issue ever
> Reign in this kingdom? (4.1.116–118)[1]

The king's concern, of course, is that his one-time friend and ally's children might rule Scotland rather than Macbeth's own children. The use of "art" here is notable, as the Renaissance use of the term points simultaneously to the work of artistic creation, as well as to what we would call magic and what we could call science or craft.

Each of the three witches announces the command "Show!" and thereby summons a series of "shadows" to appear before this small audience. These shadows are not entirely "shades," an ancient term for ghosts, however. The procession includes not only the dead but also the not-yet born. Stage directions call for *A show of Eight Kings, the last with a glass in his hand.* While the procession includes the spirit of the Macbeth's murdered friend Banquo, the "gold-bound brow[s]" of the others that pass are those of future generations. The climax of this "horrible sight," Macbeth exclaims, is when

> the eighth appears, who bears a glass
> Which shows me many more; and some I see
> That two-fold balls and treble scepters carry. (4.1.135–137)

The two orbs suggest a coronation image of James I, who could trace his lineage back to Banquo. Evocatively, the scene intermingles past, present, and future. Banquo's ghost is the phantom echo of a living man in Macbeth's recent past; Banquo's descendants are a vision of the future for Macbeth. The procession constitutes, at the same time, the past for Shakespeare's audience and also, in the case of James, the contemporaneous present. And, if Shakespeare had any sense of his own timelessness—as Ben Jonson puts it, the bard was "not for an age but for all time"—the future-vision of James represents a gaze into the past for audiences to come.

It is intriguing how this scene's primary, material object— its mirror or "glass," in Shakespeare's terms—plays an enabling role in seeing the future. Recall that the glass is held by the eighth member of the procession, and this object contains multitudes. Glass, it seems, at least in this moment in *Macbeth*, falls into the category of what Jonathan Gil Harris has described as "untimely matter" found in many Renaissance plays. These disorienting objects or materials "challenge the fantasy of the self-identical moment or period."[2] When we watch Shakespeare's play, we see a scene from the past where a character finds the future in his glass reflection. Just as Gil Harris sees this peculiar matter as "materaliz[ing] instead a temporality that is not one," the glass that Macbeth sees startlingly overlays future, present, and past in one visage.[3]

Perhaps glass has a particular propensity to link to the otherworldly. One thinks of the mirror-as-threshold for Alice in Lewis Carroll's *Through the Looking-Glass and What Alice Found There* (1871), or how *The Matrix* (Andy and Lana Wachowski, 1999) has Neo reach for a mirror only to find that it reaches for him as he leaves his quotidian world. However, it is worth noting here that glass mirrors in the Renaissance differ from our own contemporary mirrors and from mirrors in previous periods, including the medieval period in which *The Tragedy of Macbeth* is set. Pre-Renaissance mirrors were largely polished metal. The introduction of the crystal mirror in the Renaissance introduced an object more similar to our own in look and feel, yet the images produced were refracted or curved, thus not giving an accurate reflection of the physical self. And, as Deborah Shuger has shown, this led to mirrors depicted in art or literature as rarely being used for examining one's own physical characteristics.[4] Instead, mirrors are depicted where individuals view an aspirational figure, such as Christ or the Virgin Mary, looking back upon them, or they might see the future state of their face in the form of a skull staring back. These were speculative selves, one might say: that is, one aspired to be like one of these individuals in the future—if one sought the virtue of Mary, for example—or one faced the inevitability of becoming like the image in the mirror, in the case of *memento mori*.

As Alan Macfarlane and Gerry Martin have shown, medieval and Renaissance innovations around glass played a critical role in speculation—both in terms of improving human sight and in terms of positing new ideas about abstract concepts.[5] Mirrors significantly contributed to advances in geometry and in understanding causation, as well as to innovations in artistic production when used for illusion and experimenting with perspective. Recent theorizations of material culture and object studies have helped turn our attention away from the results of mirrors and to the mirror as object itself. As Sara Ahmed reminds us, objects are central to the process of orientation. She remarks, "To be orientated is also to be turned towards certain objects, those that help us find our way."[6] And, indeed, as we begin to ask which objects have particular power in our world, we should also consider her question, "What difference does it make 'what' we are orientated toward?"[7]

One of the central questions of *Glass* is why do we orientate ourselves toward glass. This scene from *The Tragedy of Macbeth*, like other depictions we've discussed in Corning's film and will encounter elsewhere, suggests we look into glass not for reflection but for speculation into the world to come or for alternate versions of the world that is.

Before we leave the Renaissance for now, let's turn to a final, intriguing mode of expression that embraces the speculative mirror. The epilogue of George Gascoigne's long poem *The Steele Glas* (1576) informs his readers that

> I shut my glass before you gaz'd your fill,
> And, at a glimpse, my silly self have spied
> A stranger troop than any yet were seen.[8]

Like the glass held by the eighth apparition seen by Macbeth, Gascoigne's text-as-glass is a site of abundance. And, importantly, it is one of speculative abundance. There is more to see here if he'd only open his mind again to write more.

Gascoigne remains speculative not only in what we might discover in the "strange troop" that populates his text but also in what future pleasures he might provide when he chooses again to write. He addresses his patron in an appeal for more financial support for his writing: "My lord, let shut the glass apace, / High time it were for my poor muse to wink," and leaves open the promise that

> But if my glass do like my lovely lord,
> We will espy, some sunny summer's day,
> To look again, and see some seemly sights.

Here, and in examples we've already seen from Corning and Shakespeare, the glass mirror is a site of future promise, and Gascoigne's text itself constitutes the very glass that the reader is invited to desire. The patron and the poet will be brought together by the experiences of gazing into glass. Reading or staring into a mirror are not isolating, narcissistic activities; rather, they inspire communication and collaboration.

In Shakespeare's and Gascoigne's imaginations, glass can look backward and forward, bringing the past world to life. While Banquo sees future generations, these are past generations for the audience. Thus, the mirror does work for the audience as well, urging them to be as good as their forebears. George Puttenham, writing a decade before *Macbeth* was probably written, posits that "no one thing in the world with more delectation reviv[es] our spirits than to behold as it were in a glass the lively image of our dead forefathers, their noble and virtuous manner of life, with other things authentic which . . . we apprehend . . . by memory."[9] Just as the mirror can speculate about the future, it can also call to the mind faces from the past. Even here, though, the mirror invokes the past to inspire us, to enliven us in the present, and to provide models for how to inspire us in future behavior.

Minority Report

The imagined propensity of glass to display the future is memorably depicted in *Minority Report* (Steven Spielberg, 2002). The film offered us the promise that individuals might one day swipe a single hand to rearrange and resize still and moving images on a glass screen. And, perhaps more importantly, some of us imagined we might feel like Tom Cruise while we'd be doing it. While our collective cultural memory of the film might most readily recall the drama of the digital asset manipulation through hand swiping, what's so resonant about what Cruise's character does in the film isn't just about the seizing and swiping that's become ubiquitous with touch-screen technologies.

FIGURE 4 Tom Cruise dials up another man's life experiences (Still from *Minority Report*, 20th Century Fox and DreamWorks Pictures).

Given that the images on the glass screen in *Minority Report* are drawn from a murderous flashpoint in someone's life, the power of the process lies in the ability to look into someone's soul. Indeed, these are insights not only into a person's inner workings but also into her or his future desires. The glass in *Minority Report* renders visible images from the near future, as the officers in the "Precrime" division attempt to stop murders before they occur.

What is the appeal of dwelling for a moment in someone else's experience? Like the purloined letters, telltale hearts, and other confessional objects that inhabit the tales of Edgar Allen Poe, the glass wall in *Minority Report* announces the libidinous impulses that simmer beneath the countenances of our friends and neighbors. Watching Cruise manipulate virtual objects on a transparent surface reminds us that glass itself is a peculiar object—one that we rarely acknowledge *as an object* because we are constantly looking through it to see something else. And ten years before the emergence of Google Glass, *Minority Report* teased us with a glass object that would respond to our whims and render the lives of others into virtual components.

The film opens with the images that will appear in the glass screen, moving from the eye of one of the "precogs" (semi-catatonic psychics who lie in a pool of water awaiting the next vision of murder-to-come) to wooden balls inscribed with the names of future perpetrators and victims. To operate the advanced technology that translates thought into screen display, pieces of seemingly data-storing glass are inserted into slots beside the display that Cruise's character manipulates. Glass isn't just a key element in these scenes in the movie, and is not solely interactive in the case of the display used by officers investigating Precrime.[10] Spielberg's world is, to borrow a phrase from Edmund Spenser's *The Faerie Queene*, "a world made of glass." In one case, it seems as if someone else is the shooter, but it ends up being a reflection of a billboard. The victim dies by being shot and then falling through glass. Cruise walks through the glass doors of a Gap store and is greeted by a holographic salesperson. The detectives gaze at the precogs through a massive glass window. Rooms are separated by moving glass partitions in the police headquarters, and people are transported by glass platforms that operate as single person elevators. Glass displays recognize characters by scanning their retinas and offer personalized marketing messages.

The glass panel that is the major focus of the opening scene represents a departure from the short story by Philip K. Dick from which the film is adapted. In the story, it's stacks of punch cards rather than images on a glass partition that give the detectives foreknowledge of the crime. When the precogs foresee Anderton (Cruise's character) committing a murder, there seems to be no doubt; thus begins the chase and the larger philosophical questions of predestiny that guide both the story and the film. At numerous times in the short-story version, we hear that Anderton has been "framed" by his rival. It's a shared term between the crime or detective genre and the technology of glass. We could say that "framing" also links to the dynamics of desire. Framing an object implies its value or draws the eye to its assumedly attractive qualities. Framing someone for a crime makes her or him desirable, as someone to capture and to pin the crime on. In turn, the process of framing someone generates pleasure for the person who gets off without punishment for the crime. Indeed, Anderton suspects— and his suspicions are reinforced by a mysterious intervener who saves his life—that the whole plot against him is driven by his wife, who he believes has taken up with a younger man and subsequently framed him for a crime he will not commit. Glass is almost entirely absent from the short story, except for a brief mention of a computer screen used for a video call. The narrative is filled with Dick's typical themes: government and military conspiracies, multiple timelines, and a bureaucracy characterized by a mix of tedium and menace.

The film touches upon issues of bureaucracy and government conspiracy but overt themes of desire are more pronounced in the narrative, dwelling in the realm of the family and the sexual. The driving psychology behind Cruise's version of Anderton, and the element that will explain why he might commit murder, is his obsession with his missing child. His son was kidnapped years before Anderton is seemingly framed for murder. In an early scene, the detective interacts with a projected film of his deceased son. Glass plays a role here, as the film is comprised of holograms projected on the wall from data stored on clear glass slides. There is seemingly nothing on the blank, transparent square of glass.

Yet it clearly stores significant amounts of data, contributing to the magical capabilities of technology delivered through glass. In several ways, the film's interactive glass operates as a multidirectional time machine. It can transport Anderton into the past, actually placing him there as he rehearses lines from the hologram as if he is there with his disappeared son. Simultaneously glass transports the child into the present— the boy never ages while Anderton re-lives high points in their time together. And glass of course can transport one into the future, in the case of Precrime. Given that it is Anderton in the images of the murder he will commit, the images also place him in the new temporal space. He sees himself looking back in the precog images in the glass. Throughout the film, the camera calls our attention to the human eye. It is Spielberg's nod to Hitchcock, and it's a way of underscoring that technology-enabled glass allows people in this future world to see more robustly. In fact, Cruise's character is addicted to a drug called "Clarity," which he buys from a man whose eyes have been removed, emphasizing that too much looking can be harmful to one's health.

The film will ultimately reunite Anderton and his wife. In her final version, the precog Agatha will foresee and describe the child Anderton and his wife will conceive in the future. The narrative thus resolves with a more just society (as the precogs will be allowed to live normal lives and the ethics of Precrime come under scrutiny), an affirmation of the couple, and the promise of procreation. The film has followed a similar trajectory as it has moved through multiple reproductive phases of reflection: first, the dead child is displayed by glass; next, Anderton is a killer; now he will be reproduced in the mind's eye of the precog through his child, who is marked by his ability to "run"—the very thing that Anderton has done throughout the film.

Microscopic vision

The story of the history of glass is one about exploration and discovery. The microscope and the telescope enabled humans to imagine other worlds and distant lands, in turn powering exploration and colonialism. Glass played a critical role in the scientific revolution because thinkers in the Middle Ages and Renaissance used a variety of glass instruments—prisms, mirrors, and lenses—that allowed for new understanding of mathematics and the operations of light. Today, glass remains an essential element to scientific experimentation and instrumentation, especially in the case of barometers, thermometers, beakers, greenhouses, and various types of lenses.

The microscope is believed to have been invented in the sixteenth century by Dutch lensmakers who experimented

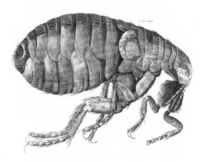

FIGURE 5 A flea never looked so captivating (Robert Hooke, *Micrographia*).

with lining up two lenses at a short distance. In the first publication of London's Royal Society, *Micrographia* (1665), Robert Hooke detailed observations made through the microscope. The book contained descriptions and illustrations of a world that had been long invisible to us: the tip of a needle, the body of a flea.

Staying up until two in the morning to read it, Samuel Pepys described *Micrographia* as "the most ingenious book that I ever read in my life." Hooke describes the microscope as opening new worlds within our own:

> By the means of telescopes, there is nothing so far distant but may be represented to our view; and by the help of microscopes, there is nothing so small, as to escape our inquiry; hence there is a new visible world discovered to the understanding. By this means the heavens are opened, and a vast number of new stars, and new motions, and new productions appear in them, to which all the ancient astronomers were utterly strangers. By this the Earth itself, which lies so near us, under our feet, shows quite a new thing to us, and in every little particle of its matter; we now behold almost as great a variety of creatures, as we were able before to reckon up in the whole universe itself.[11]

For Hooke, the telescope and microscope initiate a new age. While writers in the Renaissance revered thinkers in ancient Greece and Rome, here they are cast as "strangers" to the knowledge now available to the assisted human eye.

Hooke uses the word "new" five times in this short excerpt to heighten his readers' excitement about how with enhanced, glass-enabled vision comes the possibility of new inquiry, new stars, new creatures, and a new understanding of other worlds within and outside of our world.

Francis Bacon's unfinished utopian novel, *New Atlantis* (1627), presages the excitement of the observations made concrete by Hooke's *Micrographia*. In the story, visitors to an island civilization encounter Solomon's House, where a community of scientists engages in experiments and share knowledge. *New Atlantis* formed a blueprint for the Royal Society. A "humble admirer" of the Royal Society writing shortly after its founding suggested, "You really are what former ages could contrive but in wish and romances; Solomon's House in the New Atlantis was a prophetic scheme of the Royal Society."[12] In the use of "wish" and "romance," we can see parallels between how the admirer's description of the link between Bacon's work and the historical scientific academy points to our own fascination with how science fiction may not only predict the future but also shape our present-day desires that inform technological innovation. In Bacon's book, one of the island's inhabitants inventories the equipment shared by the scientists.[13] This inventory includes the microscope that, echoing Hooke's description, allows users to view new worlds:

We have also glasses and means to see small and minute bodies, perfectly and distinctly; as the shapes and colors of small flies and worms, grains, and flaws in gems which cannot otherwise be seen, observations in urine and blood not otherwise to be seen.[14]

In Solomon's House, prisms and mirrors also enable illusions and other special effects with optics:

We make artificial rainbows, halos, and circles about light. We represent also all manner of reflections, refractions, and multiplications of visual beams of objects.[15]

And the inventors of such things are celebrated with great prestige in

two very long and fair galleries. In one of these we place patterns and samples of all manner of the more rare and excellent inventions; in the other we place the statues of all principal inventors. There we have the statue of your Columbus, that discovered the West Indies, also the inventor of ships, your monk that was the inventor of ordnance and of gunpowder, the inventor of music, the inventor of letters, the inventor of printing, the inventor of observations of astronomy, the inventor of works in metal, the inventor of glass, . . . and all these by more certain tradition than you have.[16]

The connections implied by the chosen examples of statues are suggestive of the larger imaginative processes enabled by glass technologies. Columbus and the inventor of ships put us immediately in mind of colonial enterprises motivated by an understanding that the world was much bigger than believed and that new tools for seeing could shorten the perceived distance to reach these new regions. The inventor of glass is mentioned in the same breath as the inventor of music and letters, suggesting the ways that the arts were also inspired by innovations in glass technologies.

A startling example of a poem inspired by the imaginative possibilities inherent in microscopic vision is John Donne's "The Flea" (1633). The poem playfully taps into the power of the microscope to imagine new worlds inside tiny beings. A flea's body offers a minute physical space with the capacity to contain alternate worlds and impossible possibilities. The poem's situation is, ostensibly, a simple one: a flea has bitten both the speaker and his lover, and their blood has already commingled. Their blood mixing inside the flea both constitutes a form of sexual connection and also codifies their relationship as a near-marriage. Therefore, there remains little reason for them not to have sex. The speaker insists that the insect "is you and I, and this/Our marriage bed and marriage temple is," thus transforming the flea's body into a place where the lovers' relationship has been not only consummated but also solemnized.[17]

In addition to legitimizing what would be decidedly illegitimate in the outside world, the space within the flea also upsets normative space/time, as it both contains a marriage bed already actualized and presages a real-world marriage bed to which the speaker urges his lover. The creative logic of the space allows it to function as both persuasion and satisfaction—that way, should the real-world bid for sexual congress fail, the experience of the poem still promises the satisfaction of consummation. The spatiality of the poem is made complex and otherworldly by the claim that the two people "are met, / and cloistered in these living walls of jet," suggesting that the virtual space of the flea is large enough to contain the two lovers, their marriage bed, and a temple, but is still defined by walls that separate it from the outside world and restrict entry. Indeed, the "jet" may also imply the dark ink with which the poem is printed. The flea's virtual space exists within or parallel to the real world, but its permeable boundary can only be penetrated by the power of the lovers' desire and imagination.

The ability to see details of a flea's body is a powerful instance of enhanced sight that connects Hooke's volume and Donne's poem. It's also a breakthrough that Bacon grasps onto as a potent example of the world-discovering capabilities of glass in his philosophical treatise *Novum Organon* (1620), where he describes

> recently invented glasses which disclose the latent and invisible minutiae of bodies and their hidden configurations and motions by greatly increasing their apparent size; instruments by the aid of which the exact

shape and outline of body in a flea, a fly, a worm, and also colors and motions before unseen, are not without astonishment discerned.[18]

With the onset of the microscope, even a quotidian parasite can be transformed into an object of continual fascination for the scientist and a site of erotic potentiality for the poet. And, as Bacon makes clear, glass enables amplified sight for increased knowledge while still generating the "astonishment" that we all seek from the ecstatic experience of confronting the unexpected stranger, whether in the form of an unseen flea or a romantic interest.

Telescopic vision

Galileo did not invent the telescope, but the Italian word "telescopio" was coined for his instrument in 1611 by combining the Greek *tele*, "far," and *skopein*, "to look or see." The word migrates into English first in its Latin form, *telescopium,* in 1619 and later as "telescopioes," before being refined to "telescope." Robert Boyle, a fellow of the Royal Society and collaborator of Robert Hooke, describes "Galileo's optick Glasses, . . . one of which Telescopioes, that I remember I saw at Florence" in his volume *Seraphic Love* (1663). Galileo makes a guest appearance in a well-known allusion during John Milton's depiction of Satan in *Paradise Lost* (1667):

> the superior Fiend
> Was moving toward the shore; his ponderous shield
> Ethereal temper, massy, large and round,
> Behind him cast; the broad circumference
> Hung on his shoulders like the moon, whose orb
> Through optic glass the Tuscan artist views
> At evening from the top of Fesole,
> Or in Valdarno, to descry new lands,
> Rivers or mountains in her spotty globe.[19]

When suggesting that Satan's shield resembles the moon gazed at by "the Tuscan Artist," Milton refers to Galileo, who died twenty-five years before the publication of the epic poem. Milton's use of the phrase "optic glass" mirrors Boyle's wording and underscores that glass is at the heart of how the telescope was understood as an instrument.

The association between a divine being and the telescope testifies to the transformational power of this new instrument. The awe that new glass instruments struck in the Renaissance is projected onto how Native Americans were depicted to have perceived European explorers. As Thomas Harriot writes in his 1590 account of visiting Roanoke Island and engaging with the Native Americans there:

> Most things they saw with us, as mathematical instruments, sea compasses, the virtue of the lodestone in drawing iron, a perspective glass whereby was shown many strange sights, burning glasses, wildfire works, gun, book, writing and reading, spring clocks that seemed to go off by themselves, and many other things that we had, were so strange unto them and so far exceeded their capabilities to comprehend the reason and means how they should be made and done that they thought they were rather the works of gods than of men, or at the leastwise they had been given and taught us of the gods.[20]

Within the notion that the Native Americans saw the explorers as gods or students of gods resonates the sense that glass grants one wondrous power.

Galileo made significant improvements upon the telescope, through which the famed astronomer then made observations that upheld the Copernican model of the cosmos and undermined the Ptolemaic model. Galileo's optic glass decentered the place of the human in the universe—the stars and planets no longer revolved around the Earth. At the same time, the glass tool affirmed the powerful place of the human in the cosmos as the only mortal entity to see at great distances and "descry new Lands" (as Milton puts it). Discussions of not only new lands but also new planets, even populated ones, circulated fervently during the Renaissance. Drawing connections between literary creation and scientific discovery during the period, Roland Greene describes the realization of other worlds as "one of the constitutive elements of the early modern mentality."[21] We can see evidence of the excitement about the discovery of new worlds not only in the quotations about microscopic vision above but also in the titles of books published during the period, including John Wilkins' *Discourse Concerning a New World and Another Planet* (1638) and Bernard le Bovier de Fontenelle's *Conversations on the Plurality of Worlds* (*Entretiens sur la pluralité des mondes*, 1686). Greene's argument that early modern worldmaking produces new realms constructed "out of extant, alternative worlds" aptly befits Renaissance poets' efforts to imagine fanciful worlds that might be seen through the microscope or telescope.[22]

Fontenelle's volume describes a dialogue between the narrator and a Marquise, strolling in the latter's garden at night and observing the stars. The dialogue sums up much of seventeenth-century (and earlier) thinking regarding the existence of other worlds and even speculates that life may exist on these planets. Also meaningful for this text's role in the history of science, the Marquise actively questions and criticizes the theories put forth (Fontenelle believed strongly in education for both sexes). Also fittingly, one of the first translators of Fontenelle's volume (under the English title *A Discovery of New Worlds*) was a woman, poet and playwright Aphra Behn. The volume became a classic for women readers in England, as well as in France.[23] Behn herself was fascinated by the possibilities of other worlds and interested in positively shaping the reader's assessment of the female respondent in Fontenelle's dialogues.[24]

Milton had, in fact, visited Galileo and seen his telescope in Valdarno. Galileo's telescope simultaneously allowed him access to other worlds and brought about the dramatic shrinking of his own world. Because the Church believed his support of heliocentrism to be heresy, Galileo spent his final years under house arrest. It seems that looking speculatively can bring confinement. But dreaming of other worlds can be a means of escape even when physically bound.

Earrings and landscapes

A contemporary of John Milton, Margaret Cavendish was another poet through whose work we can see resonances of the scientific revolution and specifically, imagination spurred by the possibilities of the microscope. Her poem "A World in an Earring" (1653) envisions many worlds to be found in our world. She directs her poetic vision toward a simple piece of jewelry:

> An earring round may well a zodiac bee,
> Wherein a sun goes round, and we not see.
> And planets seven about that Sun may move,
> And he stand still, as some wise men would prove.
> And fixed stars, like twinkling diamonds, placed
> About this earring, which a world is vast.[25]

This world in a woman's earring is at first described broadly to be like our own. Each line adds to a list of what can be seen in this tiny world: cattle, lightning, thunder, plagues, mines, night, day, cities, seas, meadows, gardens, churches, and markets. We receive this information as if we are quickly surveying a map: "there nipping frosts may be," "there meadows be," "there churches be," and so on. While this long list clips by quickly, Cavendish slows the pace at the end of the poem to dilate on romantic coupling:

> There lovers mourn, yet hear them not complain.
> And death may dig a lover's grave, thus were

A lover dead, in a fair lady's ear.
But when the ring is broke, the world is done,
Then lovers they into Elysium run.

The poem combines several elements of glass that we have been tracing throughout this book. On one level, we see glass operating in its enabling capacity for sight: the speaker makes startling discoveries by peering into a microscopic world. At the same time, we gaze through the microscope and see not just the world as it is but also the world as it will be. Looking through glass speeds up time so that we see one lover mourning the other and then immediately both lovers in the afterlife, when the world ends at the breaking of the earring.

On yet another level, we see glass operating as a means of reflection; that is, peering closely at the surface of an earring reveals a world just like ours. Cavendish tells us that the world is made up of small bits or particles that are just mirror images of the larger ones of the world in which they circulate. In some ways, Cavendish's poem presages Gottfried Wilhelm Leibniz's notion of the "monadology," where small particles exist that mirror other particles. In 1698, he described this world of small mirror bits where

> each portion of matter can be conceived as like a garden full of plants, or like a pond full of fish. But each branch of a plant, each organ of an animal, each drop of its bodily fluids is also a similar garden or a similar pond.[26]

He conceived each of these bits of matter, or "monad," as a "perpetual living mirror of the universe"—as every soul is.[27]

On one more level—and here's where we come back to one of the key strands of thought about glass that we've been following—the poem is about *desire*. The final five lines of Cavendish's poem zoom in on the experience of lovers, suggesting that as we peer ever more closely at the world, we come back to the basic element of romantic desire. The scene is a profound admixture: the lovers experience desire and mourning; they are in their graves and yet they are running; a writer in a deeply Christian cultural context places her lovers in the ancient Greek, pagan afterlife, Elysium. It's a wonderful ending as the poem seems to meditate on the force of fantasy. That is, though one lover has died, we do not hear them complain. Then, even when the most apocalyptic of events might occur, "when the ring is broke, the world is done," it still opens a gateway to an idyllic space where the lovers seem more free than ever, unbound from the tiny space of the earring and entering a shared space across worlds in the afterlife. Elysium, a mirror of the earthly realm of the earring (which is a mirror of our own world), becomes visible in the microscopic vision of the poet's imagination.

Andrew Marvell's "Upon Appleton House" (1651) alludes to both the microscope and telescope, and the glass instruments are tied closely to Marvell's ability to reproduce the world in poetry. This paean to the country house estate of Thomas Fairfax likens the poet's recollection of the estate to the experience of gazing through glass. Within the "sober frame" of his poem, he depicts cattle that

> seem within the polished grass
> A landscape drawn in looking glass.
> And shrunk in the huge pasture show
> As spots, so shaped, on faces do.
> Such fleas, ere they approach the eye,
> In multiplying glasses lie.
> They feed so wide, so slowly move,
> As constellations do above.[28]

The poet's gaze operates at once as a "looking glass" or mirror, suggesting that his poem can render a pastoral scene that accurately reflects the natural world it recalls. Yet the excerpt here emphasizes that the poet can play with perspective, just as glass can. Like the magnifying or "multiplying glasses" of the microscope and the telescope, the poem makes the cattle appear as if they were fleas or tiny spots on human faces or distant planets revolving around the reader.

Like Cavendish's ability to peer into a tiny world, the invocation of glass in "Upon Appleton House" corresponds to contemporaneous fascination with methods for scientific discovery. At the same time, Marvell uses the metaphor of glass to argue for the power of poetic depiction. Later in the poem, Marvell evokes the image of a mirror to explain how nature regards itself in the country house estate:

> It ev'rywhere the meadow holds;
> And its yet muddy back doth lick,

Till as a crystal mirror slick;
Where all things gaze themselves, and doubt
If they be in it or without.
And for his shade which therein shines,
Narcissus-like, the sun too pines.

The poem reflects back the natural world of the estate like a mirror would, and the natural world itself seems to reflect upon itself. "All things" in this pastoral scene gaze into the muddy reflection in the meadow, giving a sense of subjectivity to the trees, cattle, and other elements praised in the poem. The stanza closes by suggesting that the sun sees its own reflection in the estate and longs to be with it. The poet suggests that the lens of recollection, which on the page can revivify past experiences and depict distant places, is superior to even the device-enhanced gaze of the physical eye. Indeed, Marvell's poem promises to satisfy the reader's desire for a visually enhanced experience of the world based in a blend of subjective and objective perceptions.

"Upon Appleton House" seems to tease out the implications of Horace's claim in *Ars Poetica* that "*ut pictura poesis.*" That is, "as is painting so is poetry."[29] With his use of rich sensory detail and his reference to the looking glass, the poet emphasizes how his creation can bring the country house into view. Horace explains further that "poetry is like painting. In each case, the aim in view is to be considered. A miniature should bear close inspection; a wall painting is to be seen at a distance."[30] Inspired by telescope and microscope, Marvell plays with the logics here. Rather than the reader deciding whether to examine the poem close-up or from a distance, the poet illustrates how the poem itself seizes upon multiple glasses to control from what perspective we might view its contents.

Photography

The invention of the telescope, the microscope, and the camera can be traced back to the work of early lensmakers in their efforts to improve eyeglasses. It is interesting to think about that broad (and, of course, somewhat simplified) genealogy. Glass was first used to restore eyesight to normal, healthy parameters. Then lenses were used to enable us to see much better than the best of human eyes can see. Then glass was instrumental in the design of a device that allows us to capture what the eye sees and preserve it in the photographic image. A wide array of devices that give us powerful ways of looking all rely on innovations around glass. While much has been written on the camera and on photography, we'll consider how the operations of the camera lens fall into the matrix of time, self-reflection, desire, and world-creation that this book has been tying together—and tying to our cultural fascination with glass.

When we think of the relationship between the camera lens and time, we might think of glass's function as largely retrospective. That is, the camera's glass lens seems to allow us to capture a single moment of a person's life and to later look upon what now has become a past version of that person. Or in the case of people who have died, we can see them just as they were when they were alive. But the photographic lens enables an even more complex form of looking, one that breaks down the binary oppositions between present and past, between living and dead. Indeed, photographic images expose the dialectical relationship at the heart of photography itself. On the one hand, camera images embrace Susan Sontag's suggestions that "to photograph someone is a sublimated murder" by turning subjects into "objects that can be symbolically possessed."[31] That is, we translate a *person* into a *thing* by freezing them in time on film or in a digital snapshot that can be stared upon or handled in any way we choose. On the other hand, photographic images can exemplify ways that the camera lens might function as a revivifying device. Roland Barthes, for instance, positions photography as a form of life-giving resuscitation when he gazes at a photo of his deceased mother as a young girl "at the end of a little wooden bridge in a glassed-in conservatory, what was called a Winter Garden in those days."[32] The scene of the first photograph of his mother is surrounded by glass in the same way as the image itself is captured in the frame of a glass camera lens. The garden is preserved by glass walls that make possible an artificial spring environment (with winter always visible through the walls), while the young girl is preserved by the work of the glass lens (with the viewer always at a later point in time as he reflects upon the image). The snapshot helps Barthes reach the conclusion that photography can be described as "the impossible science of the unique being," a phrase he uses to describe the way in which the photographic image preternaturally reproduces a person's unique self at a given moment.[33] As human beings, we are constantly growing, aging, and changing with each passing minute, yet the camera startlingly allows us to see who we were at a given instant.

For Barthes, the image breaks down the binary opposition between past and present because his feeble mother at the end of her life becomes "my little girl, uniting for me with the essential child she was in her first photograph."[34] Glass, once again, operates like a time machine. He is there with his mother many years ago in the Winter Garden, and the little girl is here with him to mourn his mother. Evocatively, he sees his mother as "my little girl," prompting him to reflect on the fact that he has not had children nor will he. He faces his relationship to this deceased child as presaging his "total, undialectical death" because he will not have a child "reproduced as other than himself."[35] Marjorie Perloff aptly describes Barthes' contemplation of the Winter Garden Photograph "as an elegy for his mother, as well as a kind of epitaph for himself."[36] Barthes' nuanced connection of the snapshot with reproduction—he frames himself as feeling like a father to the young girl in the photograph by gazing upon her and also as someone who realizes his own childlessness upon looking on this artificial representation of a child related to him—underscores how photography makes us uniquely aware of the operations of mortality that affirm life by foreshadowing its termination.[37] Indeed, rendering visible such paradoxes seems central to what makes photography so compelling as both an art form and an object of study for those thinking about the relationship between time and what makes us human.

We can see how the art of the camera relates to the imaginative processes we associate with glass when we think about how Barthes' contemplation of the Winter Garden Photograph echoes the sentiments about the mirror in one of Shakespeare's sonnets. Indeed, the multiple elements circulating in Barthes' discussion remix as familiar components in Sonnet 3, one of the early poems where the poet urges a young man to procreate. The poem closes thus:

Thou art thy mother's glass and she in thee
Calls back the lovely April of her prime;
So thou through windows of thine age shalt see,
Despite of wrinkles, this thy golden time.
But if thou live, remembered not to be,
Die single and thine image dies with thee.

Shakespeare urges the young man to reach the same understanding that Barthes comes to realize when confronted by the Winter Garden Photograph. The photo of the young girl allows Barthes to see the child within the face of his aging mother. It also allows him to see a reflection of his own self in her face. The realization rejuvenates both the aging woman's face and the sense of youth still dwelling inside of him. Shakespeare implores the young man to see himself as a "glass" or mirror of his mother, just as she is for him. His youthful countenance recalls her youth or "April," offering an opportunity to interpret his own appearance as "window" into her youth and his own "golden time." Just as the photo of Barthes' mother reminds him that he will die and that his self will not be replicated in a child, the addressee of Shakespeare's poem is reminded that to "die single" is to foreclose the replication of his appearance in future generations.

Shakespeare's Sonnet 3 opens, "Look in thy glass and tell the face thou viewest / Now is the time that face should form another." In some ways, Barthes' contemplation of the Winter Garden Photograph functions like a retelling or adaptation of Sonnet 3. The glass—as a mirror in Shakespeare's poem, as a photograph in Barthes' biographical prose—sparks the same anxieties, the same questions, the same longing. Perhaps Barthes' version is a bit more optimistic. He is able to understand the young girl in the photograph as a facsimile of a child of his own, and feels less pressure to have children than a man might in Shakespeare's time. Still, both depictions of encounters with versions of oneself in glass remind us that the material collapses time in ways that generate diverse responses: at times celebratory, optimistic, and brimming with expectation; at other times melancholy, maudlin, and a meditation upon what it means to be finite.

Shakespeare's sonnets

The word "glass" had multiple meanings in Shakespeare's time and, as this book argues, early contemplations of glass's real and imagined capabilities testify to the material's ongoing hold on our cultural imagination. We can see an intriguing instance of glass's multiple connotations and its power to drive fantasy in Sonnet 126, which opens with these lines:

> O thou, my lovely boy, who in thy pow'r
> Dost hold Time's fickle glass, his sickle hour,
> Who hast by waning grown, and therein show'st
> Thy lovers withering, as thy sweet self grow'st.

This poem is the last in a long sequence of poems addressed to a figure typically described as the "Young Man" or the "Fair Youth"; the poems that follow are addressed to a figure often called the "Dark Lady." The collection of 154 sonnets was first published in 1609 as *Shake-speares Sonnets. Never before imprinted.* They are believed to have been written over twenty or so years and largely circulated only among friends until finally printed when Shakespeare was forty-five years old. The first seventeen are often described as "the procreation sonnets" because Shakespeare urges the young man to have children, as we saw in Sonnet 3 above. Glass features prominently in these "procreation sonnets," as the poet deploys the mirror to suggest the appeal of producing a child.

Here, in Sonnet 126, glass is used to describe the power that the addressee has over the speaker. He holds "time's fickle glass," yet the exact nature of that glass object is ambiguous. Does the young man hold a mirror, which might show Shakespeare aging, or show the young man aging, or emphasize Shakespeare's age compared to the reflection of the young man? Or, is the glass held by the young man an hourglass? If so, we see youth as having the effect of reminding us that young beauty will fade and that we ourselves are not as young as we once were. If we imagine the object to be an hourglass, the youth is aligned with the movement of sand to mark time. Given that glass itself is generated from sand, we see yet another example of how glass comes to be associated with time in general, as well as how the passing of time can change how we see glass. The hourglass began with sand as its raw material, and later was crafted into the object that now captures sand.

In either of these cases—whether the glass contains the reflection of an aging lover or the glass controls the flow of sand to mark the aging of the lover—we see glass linked with desire. That is, the speaker depicts the young man as desirable by throwing into relief his own desirability as someone aging. Indeed, the "lovely boy" here seems to simultaneously be the speaker's beloved and the boy-god Cupid, who inspires the miserable madness of love and who is depicted in the final two sonnets of Shakespeare's overall sequence. The sonnet ultimately uses its glass object to remind us that desire and time are inextricably linked: as the young man is described as "minion of [Nature's] pleasure," all the while he is cautioned that Nature "may detain but not still keep her treasure."

The word "glass" appears ten times throughout the sonnets, and it's used toward diverse ends. In Sonnet 22, glass plays a role in recovering lost time and stimulating desire. The poem opens:

> My glass shall not persuade me I am old,
> So long as youth and thou are of one date.

The poet may gaze at himself in the mirror, but he thinks of the young man. Indeed, we might think of staring into a mirror as a narcissistic activity, but Shakespeare reminds us that we can look into the glass and see another face. Counterintuitively, the mirror becomes an object that takes us away from ourselves. In Sonnet 62, the poet admonishes himself:

> But when my glass shows me myself indeed
> Beated and chopp'd with tanned antiquity,
> Mine own self-love quite contrary I read.

He cannot understand why he would love himself and so chastises himself in the next line, "Self so self-loving were iniquity." The encounter with oneself in the mirror is an opportunity to consider how others see you and to shift one's mental gaze onto others deserving of your love.

Sonnets 5 and 6 use glass to imagine ways in which the young man's beauty might be distilled and preserved before he ages. They rest at the heart of the "procreation sonnets" and offer one in a series of arguments that seek to persuade the young man to understand the urgency of having children. The poet likens the situation to the onset of winter, when we assuage ourselves with "summer's distillation" as "a liquid prisoner pent in walls of glass"; that is, perfume trapped in a glass bottle can recall for us the fresh scents of a summer's day. Glass enables a powerful "remembrance" because

> flowers distilled, though they with winter meet,
> Leese but their show; their substance still lives sweet.

In her recent book-length study of perfume in the Renaissance, Holly Dugan notes that "olfaction, like other sensory ways of knowing, emphasizes the fungible relationship between material objects, the body, and embodiment."[38] This holds particularly true when Shakespeare fantasizes to the young man thus:

> Then let not winter's ragged hand deface,
> In thee thy summer, ere thou be distilled:
> Make sweet some vial.

The young man can be kept beautiful by preserving some part of him in his prime in the form of a child. Shakespeare chooses the metaphor of the vial because glass can be beautiful in its own right. We choose glass to contain perfume, rather than wood or metal, because it allows us to see the liquid and because the container itself can suggest the beauty one will acquire when donning the scent. Shakespeare's sonnet and Dugan's claim help us understand that glass is not solely linked with seeing as a sensory operation. In the case of perfume, glass allows a scent to be powerfully and beautifully contained, allows for a sudden release of a scent that sparks the pleasure centers, corresponds with memory, and entices for potential contact to come.

"Heart of Glass"

If we're imbuing so many qualities into glass that make it so much more than simply a lifeless object, what are our encounters with it doing to *us*? We've already heard how Susan Sontag suggests that images captured through the camera lens can turn us into objects, and we've seen how we can be reduced to snippets of experience trapped in a glass panel in *Minority Report*, or how Shakespeare muses that youth might be imagined as trapped in a bottle like perfume can be.[39]

Blondie's 1978 hit "Heart of Glass" seizes upon glass as a material most apt for describing a fragile heart. The notion of a glass heart tracks to our expression "glass jaw," where our bodies are rendered inorganic by a kind of fragility we associate with objects. The central refrain in Blondie's song tells us:

> Once I had a love and it was a gas
> Soon turned out had a heart of glass.

As lead vocalist Debbie Harry opens with these words, we're immediately keyed into the ways that passionate love can go wrong so quickly and how love has the ability engender change. The singer goes from being in love to not being in love within the space of two lines, which coincides with a shift from gas to solid. We move through time and through states of being—from an emotion that is ephemeral to a personal state of rigidity and fragility. The group's music video moves from an aerial view of New York City to the neon sign for Studio 54 to a close-up of a disco ball to Debbie Harry singing these opening lines. The song is emblematic of the '80s and has been used in films such as *54* (Mark Christopher, 1998) and *We Own the Night* (James Gray, 2007) that showcase the '80s' disco scene. We might, even playfully, imagine the disco ball as the "heart of glass" that Blondie's song laments. The "mirror ball" (actually in use since the early twentieth century) seems to embody the catastrophic effects of love gone wrong. Our eye is drawn to it and it can be a source of energy as we trip the light fantastic, yet the ball is neither the source of light nor an accurate reflection of the world around it.

We noted earlier Sara Ahmed's observation that objects play an important role in shaping who we are and how we desire because objects help us determine where we are and what we are orientated toward. We find a curious case of object orientation in John Donne's poem "The Broken Heart," which contains a vivid depiction of glass' ability to produce a speculative self, and in this case one that does not necessarily carry a positive valence. Like Debbie Harry, the speaker laments a failed romance, asking "What did become / Of my heart, when I first saw thee? / I brought a heart into the room, / But from the room I carried none with me."[40] One of Cupid's arrows strikes the speaker's heart and "at one first blow did shiver it as glass." Donne's poem closes thus:

Yet nothing can to nothing fall,
  Nor any place be empty quite;

Therefore I think my breast hath all
    Those pieces still, though they be not unite;
And now, as broken glasses show
A hundred lesser faces, so
    My rags of heart can like, wish, and adore,
    But after one such love, can love no more.

"The Broken Heart" shows us rejection's capacity to make us feel, borrowing the title of Ian Bogost's 2012 monograph on object studies, "what it's like to be a thing." Unrequited attraction can undermine the dominant position of the desiring subject because the subject is transformed into an object under the catastrophic duress of another subject's rejecting gaze. To drive his point home, Donne structures his poem to reflect shattered glass, as the easy flow of stanzas while the speaker pursues his beloved transitions into a final stanza made jagged and stilted with caesurae to coincide with the breaking of his heart. The mirror here is speculative both because it offers a glimpse into the speaker's future heartache and because it emblematizes how certain future outcomes are now foreclosed by the beloved's rejection.[41]

Glass is an object made complex by what humans project onto it. In the same way, people who are objects of our affection become screens upon which we project our desires. Blondie's song and Donne's poem underscore how we become objects when under the scrutiny of another's desire or when we feel like we've lost our subjectivity when we are rejected. New glass technologies uniquely call into question

FIGURE 6 *Rosalind Through the Looking Glass* (Philip Krejcarek, 2015).

binary distinctions between subjects and objects by blurring boundaries between humans and machines. Think of how many interactive glass surfaces are designed to respond to the natural electricity generated by the human body.

But even mirrors confuse our distinctions between the artificial and the real. Influential psychoanalyst Jacques Lacan placed glass at the center of his theory of identity formation. The "mirror stage" marks the point at which the child recognizes her reflection and understands herself as separate from others. She is rendered both a subject with a mental interiority all her own and as an object who now understands herself as available to come under the gaze of other subjects. Earlier, we said that to gaze into the mirror is to ask not only "How do I look?" but also "How will I look?" or "How will others see me?" Glass is here to remind us of our status as organic, singular beings—and of how slippery those categories can be.[42]

Sea glass

A flashpoint for locating glass at the blurry intersection of natural and manufactured is what collectors call "sea glass." These pieces of glass have washed up on shore after a few years or even centuries of circulating in the ocean. This glass formerly constituted bottles, plates, glassware, windshields, and other objects thrown overboard from ships. Thus, they "started" as human-made glass objects and are now appearing amidst sand—the substance from which those objects were originally made. The movement of the ocean rounds them into the shape of river stones, and chemical interaction with saltwater causes their frosted appearance. Sea glass is most commonly found in hues of green, brown, or white and less commonly in yellow or blue. The frequency of each color corresponds to the frequency with which that color is used in the manufacture of liquor or soft drink bottles, drinking glasses, or the many other items from which sea glass derives.

Because of its name, sea glass offers a startling instance of glass as a site of projected desire. The name implies that a piece of this substance is a piece of the sea rendered into a solid. Like the seashell collected on a day at the beach and pressed against the ear where one can hear the sound of the ocean, sea glass offers the fantasy of returning from a day at the shore with a shard of the immense body of water that one has encountered, a piece of crystallized sea dug out of the sand. Yet, this is inherent in the fantasy of glass—its simultaneously liquid and solid states—especially given that it is found where water meets land. Sea glass is also sometimes called "mermaid's tears."

Despite the name "sea glass," the sea does not *make* the glass, nor is the glass exactly constitutive of the sea. Yet, the sea does transform the glass, and the very *naturalness* of sea glass is at stake for its collectors. The North American Sea Glass Association, which hosts an annual festival and offers a newsletter for enthusiasts, states that part of its mission is

FIGURE 7 *Sea Glass with Starfish* (Jane Monahan Garrison, 2015).

to ensure that commercial members "leave sea glass in its natural state and not create imitation sea glass; meaning that their pieces are not altered by acid etching, sand blasting or tumbling." The group's logo shows a bottle floating among waves with colored stones below it. In the absence of the organization's name, one would think it was a recycling company. With the organization's name, the logo reminds us of how *unnatural* sea glass really is. Still, the romance of the glass ensures a kind of cycling—from ordinary object to something rendered beautiful to an object found by serendipity. And, indeed, shoreline restoration is also central to the association's work. Thus, beachcombers and members are acting like the sea: taking the discarded, remaking it into something beautiful, and often recasting it as jewelry, especially (Margaret Cavendish might be glad to see) into earrings.

We might see parallels to the fantasy of this glass being produced by the sea, or being remnants of the sea, in the notion that glass can be generated with lightning strikes in sand. The phenomenon is sometimes referred to as "lightning

FIGURE 8 Lightning strikes sand and engenders romance (Still from *Sweet Home Alabama,* Touchstone Pictures).

glass." Like "sea glass," the name is rich with fantasy. Such a material would offer us a remnant of something ungraspable. We can see an expression of the fantasy of lightning glass in the opening scene of the romantic comedy *Sweet Home Alabama* (Andy Tennant, 2002). A young girl and boy watch as lightning strikes the beach and then find a crescent of clear glass where the energy bolt struck. So inspired, the two share their first kiss.

The ensuing plot involves the girl (played by Reese Witherspoon as an adult) eventually finding her way back to her roots and to her childhood crush (played by Josh Lucas as an adult), who was so moved by their kiss and the transformational power of sand-into-glass that he becomes a glassblower and owns a gallery that sells glass sculpture. In real life, "lightning glass," like romance or career inspiration, is not so simple.

What are actually formed when lightning strikes sand are called "fulgurites." Far from something clear and beautiful, these are sand and rock formations that resemble stalagmites or rocky tree branches. Their formation requires a temperature of 1,800 degrees Celsius (lightning strikes typically reach a temperature of 2,500 degrees Celsius). They're not exactly ugly—they are beautiful in a strange and alien way, not in a traditionally romantic way. While the scientific name itself is rather harsh to the ear, it is derived from the Latin *fulgur*, meaning "thunderbolt." So, in some ways, the fantasy of lightning glass operates in the same way as the fantasy of sea glass: transmutation to glass allows us to capture the ephemeral, to possess a piece of something immensely powerful and uncontainable. One captures these bits of power—lightning, thunder, ocean—not only in the object named after glass but also in the image of the object captured through a glass lens. Images of fulgurites captured with a camera lens abound on the web, and a favorite mode of displaying sea glass is to place it in a Mason jar or a bottle. Looking at images of this mode of display, one might think of the phrase "lightning in a bottle." The phrase was first used in the nineteenth century, referring to Benjamin Franklin's proposed experiment from the eighteenth century, where he suggested using a kite to capture electricity from lightning, and then to store it in a glass Leiden jar. This phrase, along with variations such as "bottled lightning," has come to denote a very difficult task.

Collecting sea glass. Taking a photograph of lightning glass. Capturing lightning in a bottle. These activities focus on overlapping fantasies about glass. We imagine human-made artifacts to be profoundly natural and we connect these artifacts with the ability to contain the ephemeral. And these fantasies about glass aren't just for hobbyists or fans of romantic comedies.

Owens-Illinois, Inc. (O-I), a global glass container manufacturer, recently launched "Glass Is Life" (www. glassislife.com), a marketing campaign framing itself as "a global movement to celebrate the love we all share for glass, taste, sustainability, quality and health." The company has invested heavily in fueling consumers' love of (and fantasies

FIGURE 9 Glass is life because glass is part of Earth's life cycle ("Glass Is Life - #chooseglass" by Stu Garrett, originally taken for social content).

about) glass. Founded in 1903 as Owens Bottle Company, O-I had $7 billion in net sales in 2013, has 77 plants in 21 countries, and has over 10,000-plus product offerings.

The campaign focuses on the inherent naturalness of glass and the notion that it captures ephemeral elements from nature. Glass containers seem to be products of the natural environment and to have willed themselves into existence when we're told, "out of fire and sand, iconic O-I glass containers take shape." The idea of the glass container as part of the circle of life is reinforced by Celine Cousteau, granddaughter of Jacques Cousteau, an ocean advocate who is featured in O-I's "Glass is Life" campaign. In a video, she pours sand from a glass bottle into the wind on a beach.

In voice-over, Cousteau remarks that glass "is infinitely recyclable. Glass is good to the ocean. Glass is made from sand. Glass is natural. Glass is life." She taps into the same visceral fantasies that generate our excitement for sea glass. When we encounter a single piece of glass, we encounter the immensity of the beach and ocean.

In the same campaign, Joe Schiraldi, vice-president of brewing operations for Left Hand Brewing Company in Longmont, Colorado, says, "We don't make packaging. We choose glass." The company may not manufacture its own bottles, but the statement curiously circumvents the fact that glass packaging for beer is indeed made in a factory. The comment echoes one of the main headlines in the "Glass is Life" campaign:

> We love glass. It starts life as sand, goes through fire and magically becomes a natural, beautiful material that safeguards your food & drink and is good for the environment.

Schiraldi's claim that glass bottles are not "made" and O-I's description of fiery enchantment have resonances of science fiction author Arthur C. Clarke's famous third law: "Any sufficiently advanced technology is indistinguishable from magic."[43] Asking consumers to perceive glass as possessed of mystical properties works well for branding, even if it's somewhat nonsensical. The manufacture of glass may indeed occur through naturalistic processes, but bottles don't grow on trees.

The statement from the Glass is Life campaign, "Glass tells the truth," connects to our fantasies about glass. The campaign promises that glass "tells you that what's inside is quality." The statement simultaneously reinforces the notion that what you see is what you get, while also pointing to all of the fantasies we have about glass' magical abilities to deliver on our heartfelt desires for satiated taste.

Google Glass

In January of 2015, less than two years after distributing a limited number of prototypes to users, Google announced that it would cease production of the product it named simply "Glass." The company has promised that it will continue to work on the development of the product. Whether or not the product resurfaces and takes hold among consumers, the emergence of the product marks an important moment in the history of how we imagine glass. The product is, in many ways, speculative. It resembles something out of science fiction, and its usefulness is left largely to consumers to determine. Google Glass figures as a milestone in the history of glass not just as an innovative material object—it also brings into vivid focus how we *relate to* and *relate through* glass.

Google Glass enables the wearer to upload whatever is seen to the web instantaneously, as well as to retrieve information from the web in order to contextualize what is being seen. Unlike the "selfie," where people share moments by placing themselves in an image set in a geographical location or a social context, Google Glass reflects back to the world not the user but rather what the user sees. The product thus offers the promise of experiencing new forms of intimacy by looking not *at others* but rather *through others*.

For a product in such limited release, Google Glass seemed to be everywhere in 2014. News about the Internet-enabled eyewear frequently popped up in discussions about emergent technology and about culture more broadly. While there was a lot of chatter about Glass, people seemed to remain unsure of whether it would take off, as well as how exactly it would be used. Maybe, Google intended for us to fill in the blanks. The company's pithy marketing mini-site was made up largely of evocative images and a few brief phrases such as "record what you see" and "ask whatever's on your mind." Across the blogosphere, potential consumers extrapolated the practical applications of this technology, ranging from converting nearby conversations into searchable text to running real-time background checks on new acquaintances while flirting. Perhaps sensing that the latter application might be bad for business, one Seattle bar quickly banned customers from using the product on its premises.

In a promotional video from Google, one could see first-hand the viewpoint of someone using Glass. If all the whooping and gleeful screaming in the video was any indication, the people who use Glass will lead exciting lives—taking hot air balloon rides, rushing for last-minute flights from San Francisco to New York, strutting down the fashion runway; you get the picture. These people are following their bliss and jumping from peak experience to peak experience. But how many people are really living such lives of not-so-quiet inspiration? Abraham Maslow seemed to believe there were a select few who could attain such a high plateau of living out loud. Maslow suggested that the most highly evolved of people could reach the "self-actualization" stage of his hierarchy of needs and thereafter experience a life comprised of peak experiences. The promotional materials for Google Glass suggested that those people were out there. And, if one wasn't one of these people, one needn't worry. You could still experience such heights through their elevated eyes.

While Google Glass is less speculative than the objects in Corning's video, it still remained out of reach for most people. It was only available at first to a few users right away: those that won the company's #ifihadglass contest. A few celebrities—Neil Patrick Harris, Newt Gingrich, and Brandy Norwood—had been selected as early adopters. Andrej Karpathy, a graduate student in Computer Science at Stanford University and former intern at Google Research, has analyzed the winners of Google Glass who entered the contest by tweeting a reason to #ifihadglass.[44] Karpathy found that only 26 percent have less than 100 followers on Twitter, suggesting that these people already have a cadre of others experiencing their lives through a series of pithy headlines and news bursts. One winner, 4everBrandy, had this reason for wanting to win: "I would be sooooooo ecstatic!!!!" I'm struck by 4everBrandy's choice of wording, not because of the peak level of enthusiasm but because of the etymology of the adjective she chooses. *Ecstatic* and *ecstasy* have their origins in being "beside oneself," and the words come to us from the roots *ex-* (out of) *stasis* (place, standing). Viewing the world through someone else's eyes leads us to the highest levels of feeling and also offers the promise of stepping out of our bodies.

Yet, even people knowingly recording their own experiences can be having an out-of-body experience. The eye no longer floats naturally from object to object, but instead wearers of an intermediary lens like Google Glass look deliberately upon what they think others might want to see. Indeed, Steve Mann has coined the term "augmediated" to describe the ways that computerized eyewear shows us more of the world but also distances us from it by making us aware of the lenses that help us see the world anew.[45]

It might seem odd to use the term "ecstasy" in the same breath as Google Glass. As *Atlantic* writer Rebecca Greenfield warned, despite the stylish photos of urban hipsters on Google's site, the product might quickly lose appeal because of how dorky it looks on the wearer.[46] It's not about how Google Glass *looks*, though. Aesthetics can be fixed and beta versions are often clunky. What's exciting about Google Glass is that it invites us *to look* and makes us more aware of *when and where we're looking*. And let's not forget that there's something ecstasy inducing for those who just like to watch.

Will Google Glass be back? Will it still simply be called "Glass"? Who knows? What seems apparent, though, is that it's giving us a snapshot of a more virtual world on the horizon. And the more that everyday glass objects not only reflect but also shape our lives, the more we'll do a double take at the eyeglasses of someone we meet in a bar or at a partition in a hotel lobby. These objects might be ready to introduce us to something to get truly ecstatic about.

Trademark

By naming its product "Glass," Google seems to be trying to change our expectations of the material by claiming this basic noun (or, more nefariously, to makes its own claim about being capable of redefining an object that has been around for thousands of years). Google has even attempted to trademark the word "glass."[47]

The bid was refused by the United States Patent and Trademark Office for two reasons: "likelihood of confusion" and "merely descriptive." For the first reason, the response from the USPTO lists a series of previous attempts to trademark glass-related terms for technology.[48] The letter cites SmartGlass (Microsoft allowing communication between mobile devices, televisions, and videogame consoles), iGlass (smartphones), Teleglass (apparatus for viewing projected images), Glass3D (database management software), LookingGlass (data analysis software), and Write on Glass (a browser plug-in for enhanced customization of text and image viewing). There are also several products simply called "Glass," including smartcard technology for embedding chips in credit cards and gift cards, computer software for developing mobile applications, and an online dating service. The letter notes that those products with successfully trademarked names could be confused with Google's name in the mind of the consumer:

The registered marks are GLASS; WRITE ON GLASS; GLASS3D; and, TELEGLASS. The applicant's mark is similar to the registrants' marks. The marks all share the common feature GLASS and create the same overall commercial impression.[49]

So, the USPTO's rejection of Google's attempt to own the name "Glass" is partially based on the fact that other companies have already laid claim to this territory. Fair enough.

The second reason for rejecting the trademark bid moves us into more interesting territory. The letter states plainly that "the mark merely describes a feature or material component of applicant's goods."[50] In this, the USPTO simultaneously gets it wrong and right. The rejection seems to be based solely on the product's materiality as a form of eyeglasses with frames and lenses. To support its second justification for the rejection, the letter cites the *Collins English Dictionary*, noting that

GLASS is defined as "a hard brittle transparent or translucent noncrystalline solid, consisting of metal silicates or similar compounds. It is made from a fused mixture of oxides, such as lime, silicon dioxide, etc., and is used for making windows, mirrors, bottles, etc."[51]

The letter ultimately rejects the trademark as "merely descriptive" because of the notion that the product is primarily made of glass and falls in the "etc." category in the dictionary definition above that follows windows, mirrors, and bottles.

Yet, Google's description of Glass, which the USPTO letter cites, does not name glass material as a major component. Rather, the description focuses on the interactive functionality of the product:

> The applicant applied to register the mark GLASS, in stylized format, for "**Computer hardware; computer peripherals; wearable computer peripherals**; peripherals for mobile devices; wearable peripherals for mobile devices; computer hardware **for remotely accessing and transmitting data**; computer peripherals for remotely accessing and transmitting data; peripherals for mobile devices for remotely accessing and transmitting data; computer hardware **for displaying data and video**; computer peripherals for displaying data and video; peripherals for mobile devices for displaying data and video; **computer software**" (bold my emphasis).

Google sees its product as computer hardware and software, a device that enables production of and interaction with digital content. The USPTO justifies rejecting the company's attempt to trademark the product name "Glass" because

> the mark GLASS would be understood as describing a feature of some the goods, namely, that some of the goods

will incorporate display screens and/or lenses that are or will be made of, inter alia, glass. Accordingly, the mark is refused registration under Section 2(e)(1) as merely descriptive.[52]

Certainly, some version of the product might be sold with glass lenses affixed, but the core of the product is the frame that can be attached to one's existing eyeglasses or can be worn without them. Did the USPTO get it wrong? No. Glass, as we have seen in this book, is not just an object or a substance but also a site where, for a long time, we have sought the functionality of digital computing: access, transmission, display, and interaction.

Microsoft HoloLens

The heir apparent to Google Glass seems to be Microsoft HoloLens. Technology writers are celebrating it as superior to Google's product, especially in terms of how it better meets emergent needs. Nick Stratt, writing for CNET, describes HoloLens as heralding a moment when "Microsoft suddenly pushed us into the age of *Star Trek* and *Minority Report*."[53] The HoloLens glasses overlay holograms onto the actual world, thus perhaps even more robustly embodying what Steve Mann calls "augmediation" than even Google Glass. The idea of viewing the external world as a mix of hologram and physical terrain is not radical or new to Microsoft, but Stratt is correct that the potential for wide distribution of such a product does bring the future closer to the present. A version of the holographic effect appears in the Corning's "A Day Made of Glass" when students hold a glass pane (similar to a tablet computer) up to a forest and see a dinosaur there. In the Google Glass promotional video, an overlay of textual and pictorial information appears when one gazes at a jellyfish in an aquarium. HoloLens seems to combine but advance both concepts, in the sense that one does not need the handheld glass device in Corning's vision (the device is embedded in eyewear) and the holograms are placed more clearly on the object being observed, whereas the Google version has the information more clearly separated as a pane of a computer screen within the field of vision. In short, Microsoft's goggles offer mediated reality via pop-up visualization, powered by holograms.

Microsoft's messaging emphasizes that the goggles are not just about changing *what* we see but *how* we see. The website's headline is "When you change the way you see the world, you can change the world you see." The tagline has embedded in it not just a sense of changing our perspective but also of directing us to see in a speculative way. With HoloLens, we see the world as it might be, blended with how the world is now. The product name itself emphasizes such hybridity, with "holo" resonating with the promise of science-fictional environs and "lens" drawing us back to the early eyeglass makers who set the stage for innovations to come.

When Stratt likens the technology to what we see in *Minority Report,* he refers to the way that a user can reach out and manipulate digital assets projected in one's field of vision. He suggests that in the same way the swiping motion we see in the film predicted the smartphone, the tangibility of virtual objects seen in Microsoft HoloLens derives from the desire to be like Tom Cruise's character. The marketing site tells us that the product "goes beyond augmented reality and virtual reality by enabling you to interact with three-dimensional holograms blended with your real world." The notion that we never leave our own world separates the product from virtual reality goggles such as Oculus Rift, which offer a 3D virtual gaming experience. Oculus Rift takes you into a fantasy world, whereas HoloLens takes you into a fantastical version of your own world.

FIGURE 10 It's all about the future. A user of Microsoft HoloLens envisions his tropical vacation from the comfort of the living room. (Used with permission from Microsoft).

The difference between HoloLens and Oculus Rift is embedded in the product names. "HoloLens" implies that the eyewear lets one see the world-as-it-is blended with holograms that, based on the images on the website, already exist in the mind's eye of the wearer; "Oculus Rift" implies separation between or departure from what one would see with the eye and what one will see with the goggles. Indeed, "rift" has a violent valence to it, and this may explain why the company uses that part of the name sparingly and does not appear to include it in any of the on-product branding. The product is simply "Oculus" (the Latin word for "eye"). Microsoft's product website tells us that

HoloLens is more than a simple heads-up display, and its transparency means you never lose sight of the world around you. High-definition holograms integrated with your real world will unlock all-new ways to create, communicate, work, and play.

It is interesting that the emphasis is so much on potentiality. That is, we're reassured that what we see will be our "real world," of which we will "never lose sight." Is this a real fear for those viewing the world with digital overlays? Perhaps it is, as we'll see in the discussion below of the film *Strange Days*. But what Microsoft's goggles offer us are new ways to "create, communicate, work, and play." This seems to be the promise of the product that surpasses that of Google Glass. Suddenly, Google Glass seems so passive, so rooted in the present moment. With that product, one broadcasts for others the experiences in a given moment or discovers more information to contextualize the moment being witnessed. Here, with HoloLens, we seem to have that but also an invitation to live with one foot in the present and one foot in the next moment. Here, we see something more like Corning's "A Day Made of Glass." The world is populated by the promise of what the world could be, of the world to come. These new glasses might just allow us to live in the speculative present, to experience what we seem sometimes to imagine that glass can already deliver.

Strange Days

In an early scene in the science fiction film *Strange Days* (Kathryn Bigelow, 1994), Lenny (played by Ralph Fiennes) peddles the full sensory experience of "an eighteen-year-old girl taking a shower" to a businessman in a dive bar. In the film's speculative 1999, users of a Superconducting Quantum Interface Device (SQUID) can capture the full spectrum of sensory inputs during an experience in order to replicate it for someone wearing a SQUID device at a later time. Users of SQUID seem most interested in two forms of recorded memory, or "playback": erotic experiences and violent experiences. We hear Lenny selling a whole array of recorded sexual experiences, and we see a user watching a robbery go wrong where the original SQUID user dies. We shouldn't be surprised that snuff playback, or "blackjack," sells well. Murder, after all, is a form of peak experience. In *Minority Report,* it's the only type of crime with enough psychic force to trigger the precogs' awareness of its imminent occurrence.

SQUID technology is described as "like TV, only better" because it can deliver "life . . . a piece of somebody's life. It's pure and uncut, straight from the cerebral cortex." SQUID represents one logical extension of Google Glass, which already reflects what the user experiences in order to allow others to virtually experience the user's world. Locating SQUID as the speculative extension of Google Glass showcases the promise of new forms of connection offered by interactive glass. At the same time, it highlights the dangers of reliving the past and not being able to shift our gaze toward new (often healthier) object choices.

We see this in the film quite vividly in the case of Lenny, who is "addicted to playback." Rather than using SQUID to experience someone else's memories, he continually retreats into heightened moments from his own past. These playback sessions take him back to a time when he was in a relationship with a woman named Faith (played by Juliette Lewis).

Lenny's reliving of idyllic scenes through SQUID recalls those moments from *Minority Report* when Anderton relates to the holographic projection of his dead son just as Lenny relates to replayed memories of his lost love. These films also link to Barthes' fantasies about photography and to Shakespeare's and Marvell's fantasies about the mirror. We're always hoping for new forms of looking that might have the power to resuscitate lost beloveds.

FIGURE 11 Reliving the thrill of rollerblading with Juliette Lewis (Still from *Strange Days*, 20th Century Fox).

There is a harrowing sequence toward the end of the film, which shows the dark side of products like Google Glass or HoloLens. While Lenny's obsession with Faith has kept him from starting a new relationship, it has also fueled his sense that he needs to save her from her chaotic circumstances since their breakup. While wearing the SQUID device, Lenny sees Faith being pursued by a killer. In real time, he searches the hotel suite where he sees Faith in trouble not long ago. He simultaneously sees her being attacked in the room while he follows the action, in fear of finding her body both at the end of the playback of the recent past and at the end of his search in the present. The scene is yet one more reminder of why Lenny should have let go of Faith when their relationship ended.

Strange Days provocatively ponders what might happen when the experience of glass is replicated in the absence of glass. Cinema studies scholar Caitlin Benson-Allott suggests that Kathryn Bigelow's feature films share an interest in "often valorizing an outsider position," and the use of playback in *Strange Days* reminds us that users of illicit technology gain new intimacy with others but also risk losing their own sense of self.[54] The film also reminds us that something innocent seamlessly becomes something illicit based on who is doing the seeing. Such a concern links the world of *Strange Days* to our own world. The ease with which visual experiences are now shared online concerns parents who worry that images of their children might come under the gaze of someone with an undesired interest in them.

While the repercussions are considerable, we now live in a world where we're seeing more and more (and being asked to pay for it). What's also becoming clear is the decline in the appeal of virtual worlds such as Second Life that digitally mimic the real world. Rather, we're increasingly escaping into our own real world that's becoming more and more virtual. Using products such as Google Glass or SQUID, we can skip a few levels in Maslow's pyramid and live the life of the self-actualized by surfing between peaks actually experienced by someone else.

But are these products really something new?

It does seem that we can turn to science fiction to make sense of the present. The examples we've seen in this book align with Fredric Jameson's hypothesis that science fiction is sending back "more reliable information about the contemporary world than an exhausted realism (or an exhausted modernism either)."[55] It isn't that science fiction is showing us our future; rather, the genre is throwing the present into stark relief. William Gibson gives us another, helpful perspective on this in his collection of non-fiction essays, *Distrust That Particular Flavor*. Gibson says of his own writing, which turned from science fiction works such as *Neuromancer* (1984) to more or less realist fiction such as *Pattern Recognition* (2003) and recently returned to science fiction with *The Peripheral* (2014): "I found the material of the actual twenty-first century richer, stranger, more multiplex than any imaginary twenty-first century could ever have been."[56] The discussion thus far in this book has been an extension of these ideas while also a complication of them. The science-fictional examples certainly show how our visions of the future of glass are firmly rooted in our present-day fascination with glass as an object. Jameson's and Gibson's ideas are advanced and their claims about temporality further complicated, though, by showing that even Renaissance writers speculated that glass was imbued with qualities only now being brought to fruition by interactive glass manufacturers and producers of science fiction film.

A glass, darkly

As we have seen, glass functions as both an object and a medium through which to view other objects. In order to wrestle with glass' complex state of being in the world of objects, consider how diversely a phrase from 1 Corinthians has been translated. The book is a letter from Paul, and its thirteenth chapter is a paean on the subject of love. The King James Bible presents the line as:

> For now we see through a glass, darkly; but then face to face: now I know in part; but then shall I know even as also I am known.

The line, like the glass it describes, is opaque and dense with possible meanings. For this book's discussion, the most evocative phrase is "through a glass darkly." And, as we'll see in a moment, these four words have fascinated subsequent writers and proved a touchstone for those thinking about issues of mirroring, reflecting, identity, and desire.

The line is interesting because it describes a process where we first look through glass before we can meet someone or something directly. The King James Version is pertinent here both because it would have been the version read by many of the Renaissance writers and readers described in this book and because the version's long-reaching effects are demonstrated by the way writers have seized upon the "glass darkly" phrasing.[57] Some translations assume that the face-to-face interaction is with God. Later translations assume the glass to be a mirror. The meaning of the Greek word ἐσόπτρου is ambiguous, tracking to the word "glass" but also suggestive of a mirror, window, or lens. The use of "through" opens multiple meanings, as well. Are we seeing something anew when it is reflected back upon us? Are we looking through a window or a lens to see something we could not otherwise see? The chapter from Corinthians leaves ambiguous what we are seeing. Are we attempting to see God, our selves, or the larger world? Does "darkly" describe the quality of the glass itself, the manner in which we look, or something about ourselves as lookers?

We can explore just how potent this phrase is—for thinking about how we look, how we see what we see, how we see ourselves—by glancing briefly at its various translations since the Renaissance. The New Revised Standard Version narrows the possibility of the glass to a mirror but leaves ambiguous how obscure our vision is: "For now we see in a mirror, dimly, but then we will see face to face." The shift from "darkly" to "dimly" puts even more emphasis on the weakness of our sight, or perhaps on the limits of the knowledge we draw from looking. The American Standard Version gives us something quite similar to the King James Version, substituting "mirror" for "glass": "For now we see in a mirror, darkly." The Rheims-Douay Version places the darkness explicitly inside the viewer: "We see now through a glass in a dark manner." The New Life Version cracks the mirror, placing the fault of the incomplete vision on the glass object: "Now that which we see is as if we were looking in a broken mirror" The New International Version reads, "For now we see only a reflection as in a mirror," suggesting that we must confront ourselves before we can have direct confrontation with another.

The line is preceded by another famous line: "When I was a child, I spake as a child, I understood as a child, I thought as a child: but when I became a man, I put away childish things." In this context, we see glass being about identity, growth, transition, and change. If Paul's letter is entirely about love, then the encounter with glass points to how we mature in such a way as to prepare ourselves to relate to others, to God, and to the world. The phrase "through a glass darkly" is also about how coming to love involves passing through darkness to relate clearly and directly. At the same time, the phrase uses glass to acknowledge the darkness operating in how we look at ourselves and how we see the world.

The phrase has proven fruitful for popular science fiction and fantasy television. It figures into titles of episodes of *Highlander* (a series about an immortal sword fighter), *Andromeda* (a series about the crew of a ship led by a captain who had been frozen in time for 300 years), *Dark Oracle* (a series where fifteen-year-old twins find a comic book that predicts the future), *Haunted* (a 1960s drama series about a ghost hunter), *Lois and Clark: The New Adventures of Superman* (a series that re-tells the early days of the iconic hero), and *Millennium* (a companion series to *The X-Files* that follows investigators of bizarre crimes within the context of a secret sect attempting to initiate the end of the world in the year 2000). And it appears in canonical science fiction literature as well: Isaac Asimov gathered four of his short stories that envision the future in *Through a Glass, Clearly* (1967); Philip K. Dick modifies the phrase for his novel about a detective unknowingly pursuing himself in *A Scanner Darkly* (1977). Once more, we see glass aligned with visions of the future and questions of identity.

A 2005 *Star Trek: Enterprise* episode entitled "In a Mirror, Darkly" seizes upon the rich complexity of this phrase, depicting darker versions of the show's familiar characters. The episode is a loose prequel to a 1967 episode from the original *Star Trek* series, entitled "Mirror, Mirror." Let's begin with the episode from the original series to show how it lays the groundwork for both episodes to explore the dark nature of the characters in the reflective glass of an alternate universe. In "Mirror, Mirror," four characters are transferred into a parallel universe when an ion storm causes a mishap in the ship's transporter function. In both universes, the crew of the *Enterprise* is in negotiations with the Halkans, a peaceful race on the planet below, to obtain the planet's rich store of dilithium crystals. These colored crystals, featured throughout the incarnations of the *Star Trek* series, remind us that the future runs on glass. In "Mirror, Mirror," the switch to a parallel universe is signaled through mirroring as we see the starship *Enterprise* first traveling from left to right across the screen, then from right to left. The first clue for Captain Kirk that something is wrong is when

FIGURE 12 In the Tantalus Field, glass enables the deadliest of stares (Still from *Star Trek,* "Mirror, Mirror," Paramount Television).

Mirror Spock greets him sporting a goatee and wearing a dagger in this belt. Kirk soon hypothesizes that they have been transported to "a parallel universe, with everything duplicated . . . almost."

The mirror universe is not only brimming with potential violence—as emblematized by the dagger on Spock's belt and the use of a handheld "agonizer" to punish poorly performing crewmembers—but also charged with more overt sexual energy than the prime universe from which Kirk and the others were transported. The Mirror Sulu (with a scar on his face) grabs Uhura by the chin, asking "Still no interest?", pointing to past advances on the command deck. Mirror Chekhov attempts to assassinate Kirk to advance in rank. The characters from the prime universe, impersonating their mirror counterparts who have been transported to the prime universe, get to act out violent and erotic urges. Kirk punches a crewmember in the face. Uhura flirts with Mirror Sulu to distract him, subsequently threatening him with a knife when the ruse is over. Retreating at one point to his living quarters, Kirk is greeted by a beautiful woman lying on his bed. Marlena, with midriff bare, serves him a drink when he comes home. They share a passionate kiss. Indeed, much of the episode is a cat-and-mouse game between Kirk and Marlena in his chambers. The action of Marlena pursuing Kirk in his private space parallels the men pursuing Kirk in the public sphere. She threatens to "hunt fresh game" if he rejects her. They share more than one passionate kiss. She also introduced him to the "Tantalus Field."

At first, we understand the "Tantalus Field" to be a glass screen that allows Kirk to monitor Mirror Spock. We then learn that this device, designed by some "unknown alien scientist," allows Kirk to voyeuristically observe anyone. Finally, we learn that one press of a clear green button immediately kills whoever is being watched. "Captain Kirk's enemies have a habit of disappearing," Mirror Sulu reminds Mirror Spock at one point in the episode. Kirk gives the device to Mirror Spock as he leaves the mirror universe, in hopes that he will use it to overthrow the empire and initiate a revolution. "Tantalus Field" is a curious name for a device whose function is surveillance and disintegration. Tantalus is the name of a figure on whom Odysseus famously spies in the underworld. Tartarus punishes Tantalus by making him stand in a pool of water just out of reach of a fruit tree with low branches. The fruit is perpetually just outside the grasp of the hungry prisoner, and the water continually pulls back before he can quench his thirst. Our word "tantalize," which first appears in in English in 1597, finds its origin in this myth.

What is the role of tantalization in the episode? Perhaps the device is so-named because it suggests that sought after elements such as power or security are only one assassination away. Or perhaps "Tantalus Field" alludes to the field of vision. To spy on someone is to ultimately contemplate what it would be like to live another's life, to see what another person sees. When the *Enterprise* crewmembers return to the prime universe, Doctor McCoy remarks that he likes Spock better with a beard. Marlena's counterpart appears at the end of the episode, newly assigned to the *Enterprise*. Her first interaction with Kirk coincides with swelling music, which telegraphs the promise of a future romantic encounter. He describes her as a "nice likeable girl," adding, "I think we could become," he hesitates, "friends." Should Spock grow a beard? Will Kirk and Marlena have a fling? Earlier in the episode, McCoy reels at the encounters with the sinister, decadent versions of their colleagues. He asks, "What kind of people are we in this universe?" No one answers, but the obvious answer is: "You are yourselves." The episode "Mirror, Mirror" presents the characters acting out desires and interactions already simmering beneath their more benevolent exteriors in the prime universe. And, if the title echoes the evil queen's mantra in *Snow White*, we see the confrontation with mirror-selves as an encounter with a more desirable form of oneself.

Throughout the episode, we only briefly hear about the mirror counterparts in the prime universe. The imposters were immediately thrown into the brig. Mr. Spock explains, "It was far easier for you, as civilized men, to behave like barbarians than it was for them, as barbarians, to behave like civilized men." It seems that virtuous people can convincingly pretend at dark desires, but the reverse is not possible. It opens the question: In our face-to-face meeting after gazing into the glass darkly, do we embrace our inner barbarian or do we advance to a more civilized version of ourselves?

The 2005 *Star Trek: Enterprise* episode, "In a Mirror, Darkly," takes place in the same alternate universe but does not involve characters from the prime universe switching over. We obtain a broader sense of how this whole universe is inherently corrupt as the opening credits show scenes of military action and domination. Scott Bakula, who normally plays Captain Archer on the show, is second-in-command of the *Enterprise*. Hoshi Sato, the communications officer from the regular series, is the lover of the mirror-captain. She's slinking around in sexy lingerie just as Marlena was in "Mirror, Mirror," and the female crew uniforms show off bare midriffs. Moments after Mirror Archer overthrows the captain, Mirror Sato flirts with the new captain in his quarters. Mirror Archer's dog growls and we get the sense that even he is evil. "Whatever belonged to the previous captain is yours for the taking," the communications officer tells her new captain. They share a passionate kiss before she tries to stab him with a knife hidden in her skimpy top. Later, we see them sweaty and post-coitus talking politics in bed. Part of the thrill of these episodes in the mirror universe is that viewers can imagine erotic pairings not present in the more sanitized prime universe. It's a fantasy about the fantasy. It's slash fiction with high production value. In fact, we get to see Mirror Archer and Mirror Sato in bed several times in steamy scenes, though she does end up poisoning him. He, dying and shirtless, looks on while she shares a sexy kiss with the security officer who helped her. We're moving through fantasy scenarios quickly now. First, a scene with hints of erotic cuckolding, then on to a scene of imperial domination. The communications officer takes the captain's chair and declares herself "Empress Sato" at the end of the episode.

At their most overt level, the mirror universes in these episodes seem to operate as cautionary tales. Decadence, expressed as a lust for power and for erotic coupling, is offered as the dark side to the deeply democratic, egalitarian, and polite future embodied by the United Federation of Planets to which the prime universe characters belong. However, the characters in the original series are left longing for shades of the potentiality they glimpsed in the mirror to come to life in their world. And we, as the audience who has gazed upon these dark counterparts, can't help but long to see more of them. The brief glimpse through the mirror leaves us wondering if we've had a vision of the potentiality of these individuals, a hint of face-to-face meetings to come.

Surfaces

When Microsoft chose the name "Surface" for its tablet computer, the company clearly tapped into the magic of what such a device offers. As an object, a tablet looks like a small, thin rectangle with a glass screen on one side. As a device, though, this object troubles our sense of surface and depth. On the one hand, the device is *all surface*; it's just a thin pane covered by non-transparent glass. On the other hand, the device is *all depth* because it enables our access to endless mines of information and experiences. The name is also particularly compelling because surfaces in general increasingly comprise the places we expect to find interactivity.

Glass table surfaces, for example, are quickly becoming populated by interactive technologies. While wireless connections have made the sight of a food server in a restaurant taking an order on a tablet device not uncommon, consumers are now ordering their food through the table itself. Such an experience draws a tighter connection between the virtual experience of food on a (digital) menu and the food itself, placed on top of the very surface where the food was displayed. Inamo Restaurant in London's Soho neighborhood, for example, has its menu projected on the surface of its glass tables. The restaurant's website promises that visitors can "set the mood [by choosing their preferred tablecloth], discover the local neighbourhood, and even order a taxi home."[58] In addition

FIGURE 13 The Nervana "ghost wall" (Still from promotional video, Nervana Group).

to bridging the space between imagination generated by the menu and the actual arrival of food to the customer, the glass brings the local world and the near future to the user's fingertips.

Walls are also quickly becoming more than separators of rooms. Chicago-based company Nervana uses the term "ghost wall" to describe the interactive partitions it installs in businesses such as the Hard Rock Hotel and Swissotel in Chicago.

At the Hard Rock Hotel, the wall offers information about hotel services and nearby shopping. It is difficult to know what is being *ghosted* here—the information in the wall or the outdated notion of a wall as a non-interactive surface. In Miami, a building simply named "Glass" will be an exclusive luxury condo building eighteen stories high with only ten residences. It will be located in Miami Beach in the trendy South of Fifth neighborhood. Prices for the units start at $7 million and go up to $35 million for the three-floor penthouse. Average prices for the building are around $9 million, and it is scheduled to be completed in 2015. The lobby will feature interactive, floor-to-ceiling glass walls, and the stated goal is to integrate indoor and outdoor living. The speculative images of the building on the developer's website leave the interactive walls pixilated, thus inviting potential owners to project their own desires onto what these partitions may deliver.

Glass in automobiles has become a surface onto which we project our fantasies of interactivity and upon which interactive technologies are increasingly delivering information. We saw a glimpse of this in the Corning film, where the glass dashboard plans the route and could project themed imagery. Windshields, too, are surfaces where we envision finding digital information. The interactive, multi-touch windshield on a car makes its way into two recent films: *Mission Impossible—Ghost Protocol* (Brad Bird, 2011), and *Captain America: The Winter Soldier* (Anthony Russo, Joe Russo, 2014). These action films confirm our expectations that glass objects should offer portals to interactive experiences. Characters encounter the windshields during high adrenaline moments—chases, attacks—and the glass becomes the rational surface that responds at the speed of thought. It is simultaneously the site of precarity, in that it would break at any moment, and the site of defense, because it directs the user to desired location and to safety. The more we see big-screen stars interacting with intelligent glass, the more we ourselves expect that glass surfaces should recognize our presence and invite us to handle the virtual objects displayed within.

In *Ghost Protocol,* Ethan Hunt (Tom Cruise, once more living in a speculative world at his command) and a fellow super spy access an interactive, multi-touch car windshield to dynamically plan a faster route as they drive through the crowded streets of Mumbai. The scene illustrates the fantasy that Tom Cruise and Paula Patton can simply reach out and touch a nearby object, demanding that it awake and respond to their command.

The feature isn't all fantasy, though. It's based on BMW's ConnectedDrive technology, which "enables drivers to integrate data from the car, driver and surroundings with an all-encompassing network of interactive information."[59] BMW's future is all about glass. The company's Vision

FIGURE 14 A new level in cars that promise "responsive handling" (Still from *Mission Impossible—Ghost Protocol,* Paramount Pictures).

EfficientDynamics concept car is comprised of mostly large glass surfaces, giving the driver an even more immersive experience of the road.

The firmness of glass and the ways that we've come to appreciate it for its ability to protect us is embedded in the term "windshield," a name that seems to have initially been used for bicycles and for coats and then first applied to cars in a 1911 advertisement in the *New York Times* for a "Speedwell 1911 four-passenger, semi-racer . . . extraordinary equipment includes top, windshield, shock absorbers." Though certainly the glass in cars shields passengers from the wind, we also think of windshields as fields enabling access to the world in front of us rather than protecting us from it. The automobile is, after all, an object that enables the fantasy of travel, whether that fantasy is about getting from one place to another or transporting ourselves to a safer, more sexy self through acquisition of a new car.

In *Captain America: Winter Soldier*, Colonel Nick Fury (played by Samuel L. Jackson) is attacked by unknown agents while driving his SUV; the windshield plots escape routes, hosts video chat, reports on functionality of car systems, and even assesses Fury's medical condition.

It would seem like the stuff of science fiction if it weren't simply mixing extant technologies such as Google Glass, Microsoft HoloLens, and Fitbit. The notion of auto glass as interactive is already a reality. At the 2012 Chicago Auto Show, a Mazda car on display featured an Interactive Window powered by Fusion92's VisionTouch technology, allowing

FIGURE 15 The interactive windshield has you covered (Still from *Captain America: Winter Soldier,* Walt Disney Studios).

for entry into a sweepstakes directly in the car window. The window, while fully functional as an interactive surface, remains speculative in (at least) two ways: the contest entry allows the user to dream of owning the next year's model of the car; placing the digital entry form in the window itself allows the user to fantasize about car functionality previously only seen in science fiction films.

In our fantasy worlds, it seems second nature for our heroes to find glass in their environments ready to respond to them. Robert Downey Jr.'s alter ego Tony Stark, when not running a global conglomerate or driving a race car in Monte Carlo, can simply touch a free-standing glass panel in his lab for a view of phantom components of devices. As we see at the end of *The Avengers* (Joss Whedon, 2012), the visor that covers Iron Man's face is capable of both monitoring the atmosphere and making a videophone call to his girlfriend. In *The Amazing Spider-Man 2* (Marc Webb, 2014), Harry Osborne is surprised when he activates his glass desk to discover it interacts with other objects to retrieve stored digital data. These examples showcase the desirability of responsive glass as we see celebrities or superheroes increasingly interacting with and through glass. Yet, as with the examples above, science fiction is looking more like the present every day. Car manufacturer Scion's "ghost glass" business cards interact with other smart glass surfaces in the showroom to display virtual auto details, as if the cards themselves contain specters of physical objects housed elsewhere in the organization. Interactive glass manufacturers are utilizing the term "ghost" to describe their products, paradoxically emphasizing that emergent forms of glass will make the ephemeral physical but also stressing that interactive glass replaces outmoded, non-interactive physical barriers.

Work done by theorists of objects and material culture is not only helping us understand changes in our larger culture but also shaping those changes.[60] For example, interactive glass instantiates what Arjun Appadurai has named the "mediascape," a conceptual component of the cultural imaginary across which culture is produced. Intriguingly, a US-based firm that specializes in 3D surface projection and interactive walls emerged shortly after Appadurai coined the term, and named itself "Mediascape Corporation." When we take glass as the focus of an object lesson, we see not only future and present collapsing within our case studies but also theory and practice.

"A World of Glass"

Glass is an object or substance that we all encounter constantly. Historically, we have expected to look through glass at something else or, in the case of a mirror, expected it to reflect our own image. Interactive glass is seemingly changing the nature of this object. When we examine depictions of glass since the Renaissance, we realize how we have long been drawn to this ubiquitous object to serve our increasing desires to be stimulated by inanimate objects and to be responded to by such objects. We will end by turning our attention to the past once more.

The word "glass" comes to us from Old English, and the earliest recorded use of the term in English is around the year 888, in King Alfred's translation of Boethius' *The Consolation of Philosophy* from Latin into vernacular Old English. The *Oxford English Dictionary* suggests that the ultimate root of the word "glass" may be Germanic, *glǎ-* or *glǣ-*, a variant of *glô-*, to shine. In this etymology, the name for the object or material *glass* is directly related to the effects of glass. *To shine* enables something to stand out, to look new or promising. *To shine* something means to make it look like new or make it look its best. Glass, it seems, has for a long time been about desirability. Genealogies are rarely simple, however. Starting in 1547, "glass" appears to have circulated as an adjective that indicated the color gray. This form of the word may come from the Welsh *glas*. The etymology suggests another operation of glass, which paradoxically is at the heart of the material's operations as well: to see something as gray renders it innocuous. And this certainly connects to the way we often don't see glass. Indeed, its very role is to be unnoticed. Think of drinking glasses, computer screens, windows, and eyeglass lenses. Glass exists simply to *not* exist, to allow transparency or access to things within or beyond it.

The two etymologies are not necessarily contradictory. As noted in the discussion of the sonnets, in Shakespeare's time "glass" was used as a verb meaning to enclose in glass. It could also mean to place an object in front of a mirror. To enclose something in glass is at once to showcase it for viewing and to preserve it at its best. Glass makes its contents shine by making us not notice the glass itself.

Let us turn one final time to the literature of the Renaissance. In the third book of Spenser's *The Faerie Queene* (1590), the heroine Britomart encounters Merlin. The wizard possesses a "charmed looking glass," which he uses to show the knight her destiny to marry her missing paramour.[61] The moment conflates many of the functions of glass that we've seen throughout the book. The device allows Britomart to access the future, to determine a focus of her romantic desire, and to render someone as an object that might be possessed.

The scene occurs in a fantasy world with dragons, wizards, and knights. At the same time, it's a world that parallels advances in Elizabethan England, where innovations in glass were allowing individuals to see at a great distance and to suggest to others that they possessed god-like knowledge. Spenser tells us that Merlin had devised

> By his deepe science, and hell-dreaded might,
> A looking glass, right wondrously aguiz'd,
> Whose virtues through the wide world soon were
>   solemnized.
> It virtue had, to show in perfect sight,
> Whatever thing was in the world contained,
> Betwixt the lowest earth and heaven's height,
> So that it to the looker appertained;
> Whatever foe had wrought, or friend had feigned,
> Therein discovered was.

Merlin's magic glass contains everything that the world contains, and its applications are myriad. When Britomart gazes into it, she looks for her own reflection but cannot find it. Then, she shifts her gaze to look for who might be her future husband. Love is the link that moves her away from the narcissistic gaze and toward someone who could fulfill her desires. Then, a "comely knight" appears. Merlin's glass also has military applications. Predicting the Tantalus Field we encounter in the *Star Trek* mirror universe or the glass display in *Minority Report*, Spenser describes the glass as able to identify and nullify foes at a distance. In both the science fiction narratives and the Renaissance poem, glass is powerful because it is capacious. Spenser describes Merlin's mirror as simply "round and hollow shaped," yet it holds all. The mirror appears

> like to the world it selfe
> and seemed a world of glass.

The notion that glass could contain the world, or that the world could be understood as simply a glass, abounded in the Renaissance. We've seen how Margaret Cavendish imagined an entire world in an earring and how Andrew Marvell likened an entire landscape to a mirror in which the sun saw its reflection. We might also think about how Hamlet puts on a play to "hold the mirror up to nature." Glass proves the best metaphor for how art mimics life, and later Hamlet tries to jar his mother to her senses when he confronts her with "a glass / Where you may see the inmost part of you."[62] Recall that O-I's "Glass is Life" campaign claimed that "glass is truth." Spenser, Shakespeare, and other Renaissance writers seemed to believe that the object's capacity to hold all and to reveal all could prove such a claim true.

Postscript: What's in my pocket?

I have always loved the first exchange between Bilbo Baggins and Gollum in J. R. R. Tolkien's *The Hobbit* (1937). The two ask each other a series of riddles. Tolkien was a scholar of medieval literature, and several of the riddles he includes in his book come from a manuscript that dates back to the tenth century. The *Exeter Book,* an anthology of Anglo-Saxon poetry, contains almost one hundred riddles, or *enigmata*, but it doesn't contain the final riddle that Bilbo poses to Gollum. The hobbit asks, "What have I got in my pocket?"

The question infuriates Gollum. How could he possibly know?

Right now, in my pocket, I have my iPhone. I'd guess that, either right now or at some point recently, you've probably had a smartphone in your pocket. By 2020, 80 percent of adults *globally* will own a smartphone connected to the web.[63]

The iPhone and other similar devices represent one of the most ubiquitous forms of glass with which we interact. And we interact with it in all sorts of ways. On a tactile level, we're constantly tapping or swiping the screen. On an interactive level, we're seeing ourselves, seeing others, or looking for something in the screen. On an emotional level, we alternate between fretting about and ignoring this piece of glass. But it's always there. It's a portal. It's a window. It's an access point. And perhaps it's not until the screen shatters or cracks that we're reminded that the device is glass.[64]

Maybe the coming world is a world made of glass—and not just in the ways that Corning and other technology companies imagine, where glass surfaces are always within reach and always interactive. We need to remember that the world we access through these glass surfaces is also constituted from glass. The information that populates our screens is powered by circuit boards and a global wired network made from fiberglass. This material was created to replace failing copper wire in the phone system, and it was Corning that developed a form of clear glass that could carry light: fiber optics. Glass, in the form of fiber optic cable, connects the strands of the web that delivers to the user whatever she or he desires.

The iPhone and the Internet give us final examples of how the Renaissance's fantasies about glass are our own. In everyday glass objects, we see reflected the shared human imagination that imbued glass with interactive qualities, whether in lyric poetry, on the showroom floor, or in a science fiction film.

Further reading

There have been a number of books published in the last twenty years that examine the history of glass. A small number of books explore depictions of glass—particularly mirrors—in literature. There also have been many books published that examine the history of glass as a decorative or functional object. Traditional studies of glass focus on the craft of glassmaking, particular periods in development of ornate glass forms, or broader histories of the importance of glass in culture. Thus, texts such as *Glass: A World History* (University of Chicago Press, 2006) by Alan Macfarlane and Gerry Martin, or David Whitehouse's *Glass: A Short History* (Smithsonian Press, 2012) will appeal to readers seeking to trace the unique history of glass in culture. Significant work has been done on the mirror as an ornate object, as part of a household, and as a material whose manufacture has become increasingly sophisticated. One of the most prominent examples is Sabine Melchior-Bonnet's *The Mirror: A History* (Routledge, 2002).

Several books have examined representations of glass in early English literature, including Herbert Grabes' *The Mutable Glass: Mirror-Imagery in Titles and Texts of the Middle Ages and English Renaissance* (Cambridge University Press, 1982) and Edward Nolan's *Now through a Glass Darkly: Specular Images of Being and Knowing from Virgil to Chaucer* (University of Michigan Press, 1991). Rayna Kalas' *Frame, Glass, Verse: The Technology of Poetic Invention in the*

English Renaissance (Cornell University Press, 2007) offers a fascinating discussion of how advances in glass technologies offered a vocabulary for poets thinking about their craft in Shakespeare's time. In some ways, my book most closely shares an approach with Benjamin Goldberg's *The Mirror and Man* (University of Virginia Press, 1985), which showcases scholarly research on the ancient, worldwide mythologies concerning mirrors and the uses of mirrors in technology of the second half of the twentieth century. Some readers might also be inspired by a 2013 volume from Punctum Books, *Transparent Things: A Cabinet* (eds. Maggie M. Williams and Karen Eileen Overbey), which collects a series of essays on medieval scholarship and pedagogy. The volume is positioned as a "love letter" to the Material Collective, a collaborative of art historians and students of visual culture that seeks to foster new thinking about objects, and some of the essays frame their discussions using transparent objects such as crystals and stained glass.

ACKNOWLEDGMENTS

Various individuals played a role in bringing this book to fruition, whether urging me to be part of the Object Lessons series, talking through various parts of the argument, or simply passing along an interesting reference to glass. I extend thanks to Bryan Alexander, Amanda Bailey, Chris Bates, Ian Bogost, Gina Caison, Marcus Ewert, Margaret Ferguson, Jeffrey Fisher, William Garrison, Jane Monahan Garrison, Stephen Guy-Bray, Scott Hendrix, Mary Holland, Philip Krejcarek, Marina McDougall, Colin Milburn, Haaris Naqvi, Kevin McMahon, Gregory Marks, Christopher May, Kyle Pivetti, Helen Saxenian, Christopher Schaberg, Karl Schmieder, and Molly Walsh. An early version of this book appeared as an article in *The Atlantic,* and I am grateful to the magazine's editorial staff for inviting me to share nascent thinking about this project.

NOTES

Preface

1 Alan Macfarlane and Gerry Martin, *Glass: A World History* (Chicago: University of Chicago Press, 2002), 10–16.

2 All discussions of word meanings and origins in this book cite the *Oxford English Dictionary* online, http://www.oed.com.

3 The Renaissance period witnessed a dramatic increase in literary discussions of glass. Margaret Ezell notes an "alarming" increase in texts about mirrors and glass in the seventeenth century, with 185 texts with mirror titles published between 1640 and 1660 alone. Margaret J. M. Ezell, "Looking Glass Histories," *Journal of British Studies* 43, no. 3 (July 2004): 320–21.

Chapters

1 For quotations from Renaissance texts in this book, I have modernized the spelling. All references to Shakespeare's work are drawn from *The Norton Shakespeare*, eds. Stephen Greenblatt, Walter Cohen, Jean E. Howard, and Katharine

Eisaman Maus (New York and London: W. W. Norton & Company, 2008).

2 Jonathan Gil Harris, *Untimely Matter in the Age of Shakespeare* (Philadelphia: University of Pennsylvania Press, 2008), 189.

3 Ibid.

4 Deborah Shuger, "The 'I' of the Beholder: Renaissance Mirrors and the Reflexive Mind," in *Renaissance Culture and the Everyday*, eds. Patricia Fumerton and Simon Hunt (Philadelphia: University of Pennsylvania Press, 1999), 21–41.

5 Alan Macfarlane and Gerry Martin, *Glass: A World History* (Chicago: University of Chicago Press, 2002),

6 Sara Ahmed, *Queer Phenomenology: Orientations, Objects, Others* (Durham, NC: Duke University Press, 2006), 1.

7 Ibid.

8 George Gascoigne, *The steele glas. A satyre co[m]piled by George Gascoigne Esquire. Togither with The complainte of Phylomene. An elegie devised by the same author* (London: Henrie Binneman for Richard Smith, 1576), lines 1132–34.

9 George Puttenham, *The Art of English Poesy: A Critical Edition*, eds. Frank Whigham and Wayne A. Rebhorn (Ithaca and London: Cornell University Press, 2007), 129.

10 Companies such as Samsung, Planar Systems, and Lumineq are offering transparent displays like the ones depicted in the film. One of Samsung's displays is called "Smart Window," directly implying an ontological claim to intelligence on the part of the glass. The product uses sunlight, rather than electrical lighting, to keep the display backlit. Planar and Lumineq are developing "heads-up displays" which sit within the viewer's line of sight and provide information about what the viewer is seeing. For example, the transparent display might sit at the base of an auto windshield and display information such as speed, traffic, or upcoming obstacles. As we'll see, such displays are built into the windshields themselves in *Mission Impossible III* and *Captain America: The Winter Soldier*. Such displays would feel right at home in Corning's "A Day Made of Glass."

11 Robert Hooke, *Micrographia: Or Some Physiological Descriptions of Minute Bodies Made by Magnifying Glasses with Observations and Inquiries Thereupon* (London: Jo. Martyn and Ja. Allestry, 1665).

12 Joseph Ganville, *Scepsis Sientifica Or Contest Ignorance, the Way to Science; in an Essay of the Vanity of Dogmatizing, and Confident Opinion, with a Reply to the Exceptions of the Learned Thomas Albius* (London, 1665; reprint, London: Kegan, Paul Trench & Co., 1885), 125.

13 The Royal Society was probably born more out of necessity than out of fantasy. Telescopes and microscopes, as well as other scientific equipment needed to discover these invisible, new worlds, were expensive. Lorraine Daston and Katharine Park suggest that "natural philosophy was sociable because it had become collaborative, and it had become collaborative not only because it had become factual, but also because no Maecenas had appeared to foot the bills for assistants and equipment." Lorraine Daston and Katharine Park, *Wonders and the Order of Nature: 1150–1750* (New York: Zone Books, 2001), 245–46.

14 Francis Bacon, *The Major Works*, ed. Brian Vickers (Oxford: Oxford University Press, 2002), 484.

15 Ibid., 485.

16 Ibid., 487.

17 John Donne, *The Complete English Poems* (New York: Penguin,

1996), 58–59.

18   Francis Bacon, *The New Organon*, eds. Lisa Jardine and
Michael Silverthorne (Cambridge: Cambridge University
Press, 2000), 171.

19   John Milton, "Paradise Lost," in *The Norton Anthology of English
Literature Volume B: The Sixteenth and the Early Seventeenth
Century*, eds. Stephen Greenblatt, Katharine Eisaman Maus,
George Logan, and Barbara K. Lewalski (New York and
London: W. W. Norton & Company, 2012), 1945–2175.

20   Thomas Harriot, *A Briefe and True Report of the New-Found
Land of Virginia*, ed. Paul Hulton (New York: Dover, 1972),
375–76.

21   Roland Greene, "A Primer of Spenser's Worldmaking:
Alterity in the Bower of Bliss," in *Worldmaking Spenser:
Explorations in the Early Modern Age*, eds. Patrick Cheney
and Lauren Silberman (Lexington: University Press of
Kentucky, 2000), 9.

22   Rayna Kalas has shown that Renaissance poets seized
upon themes ranging from "framing" to "perspective" to
"reflection"—in order to talk about the poetic process.
Indeed, the term "poetry" comes to us from the ancient
Greek term for making: *poesis*. The making of a poem, then,
corresponded with the technical and material operations of
building and craftspersonship, especially in terms of working
with the material glass. Rayna Kalas, *Frame, Glass, Verse:
The Technology of Poetic Invention in the English Renaissance*
(Ithaca and London: Cornell University Press, 2007).

23   Fontanelle, Bernard le Bovier de, *Conversations on the Plurality
of Worlds*, ed. Nina Rattner Gelbart, trans. H. A. Hargreaves
(Berkeley: University of California Press, 1990), xxix.

24   See Margaret W. Ferguson's "'With All Due Reverence and

Respect to the Word of God': Aphra Behn as Skeptical Reader of the Bible and Critical Translator Fontenelle," in *Reading Women: Literary Authorship and Culture in the Atlantic World, 1500–1800*, eds. Heidi Brayman Hachel and Catherine E. Kelly (Philadelphia: University of Pennsylvania Press 2008), 199–216.

25 Margaret Cavendish, *Paper Bodies: A Margaret Cavendish Reader*, eds. Sylvia Bowerback and Sara Mendelson (Orchard Park, NY: Broadview Press, 2000), 253–54.

26 Gottfried Wilhelm Leibniz, *The Monadology*, trans. Robert Latta (Ithaca: Cornell University Press, 2009), section 67.

27 Ibid, section 56 and section 77.

28 Andrew Marvell, "Upon Appleton House," in *The Norton Anthology of English Literature Volume B: The Sixteenth and the Early Seventeenth Century*, eds. Stephen Greenblatt, Katharine Eisaman Maus, George Logan, and Barbara K. Lewalski (New York and London: W.W. Norton & Company, 2012), 1811–33.

29 Horace, *Satires, Epistles, and Ars Poetica*, trans. H. Rushton Fairclough (Cambridge, MA: Harvard University Press, 1942), 443.

30 Ibid., 447.

31 Susan Sontag, *On Photography* (New York: Picador, 2001), 14–15.

32 Roland Barthes, *Camera Lucida: Reflections on Photography*, trans. Richard Howard (New York: Hill and Wang, 1982), 67.

33 Barthes, *Camera Lucida*, 69.

34 Barthes, *Camera Lucida*, 72.

35 Barthes, *Camera Lucida*, 72.

36 Marjorie Perloff, "'What has occurred only once': Barthes' Winter Garden/Boltanski's Archives of the Dead," in *Writing the Image After Roland Barthes*, ed. Jean-Michel Rabate (Philadelphia: University of Pennsylvania Press, 1997), 41.

37 Barthes, *Camera Lucida*, 72.

38 Holly Dugan, *The Ephemeral History of Perfume: Scent and Sense in Early Modern England* (Baltimore, MD: Johns Hopkins University Press, 2001), 19.

39 It is interesting that in the Renaissance, "glass" operated as verb meaning "to protect by a covering of glass, to enclose or case in glass." The *Oxford English Dictionary* credits Shakespeare with the first use of the word in this way, as desirable eyes in *Love's Labour's Lost* (1598) are likened to "jewels in crystal for some prince to buy" as the viewer becomes increasingly curious about these jewels and "where they were glass'd" (2.1.244–245).

40 Donne, *Complete English Poems*, 46–47.

41 Once more, Rayna Kalas' argument that glass offered a powerful heuristic device that was seized upon by early modern poets has purchase here. I believe we can see an instantiation of Kalas' argument in Donne's poem, as well as an example of what Samuel Daniel describes in his 1603 *Defence of Ryme*: that "All verse is but a frame of wordes confined within certain measure," a claim which Kalas interprets to indicate that "the musical and lexical harmony of the world's frame manifests itself in verse." Daniel, *Defence of Ryme*, 2: 359 and Kalas, 59.

42 John Dee, a mathematician and astronomer who advised Elizabeth I, depicts vividly how a figure in the mirror confuses our senses and our idea of a single, organic self. He advises, "If you, being (alone) near a certain glasse, and proffer, with dagger or sword, to foin at the glass, you shall suddenly be moved to give back (in manner) by reason of an Image, appearing in the air, between you & the glass, with like hand, sword or dagger, & with like quickness, foining at your very eye, likewise as you do at the Glass." John Dee, "To the Unfeigned Lover of truth, and constant Students of Noble *Sciences*," in *The Elements of Geometrie of the Most Auncient Philosopher Euclide*, trans. Sir Henry Billingsley (London, 1570), sig. bijr.

43 Arthur C. Clarke, "Hazards of Prophecy: The Failure of Imagination," in *Profiles of the Future: An Enquiry into the Limits of the Possible* (New York: Harper and Row, 1973), 36.

44 http://cs.stanford.edu/people/karpathy/glass/.

45 Steve Mann, "My 'Augmediated' Life: What I've Learned From 35 Years of Wearing Computerized Eyewear," *Spectrum*, March 1, 2013.

46 Rebecca Greenfield, "Don't Hate the Dorks, Hate the Glass," *The Atlantic* (May 3, 2013), http://www.thewire.com/technology/2013/05/google-glass-design/64860/.

47 Jacob Gershman, "Google Is Having Trouble Trying to Trademark the Word 'Glass,'" *Wall Street Journal* (April 3, 2014), http://blogs.wsj.com/digits/2014/04/03/cracks-in-googles-bid-to-trademark-glass.

48 John Dwyer, letter, USPTO to Google (September 18, 2013), http://online.wsj.com/public/resources/documents/googleglassuspto.pdf.

49 USPTO to Google, p. 3.

50 Ibid., 4.

51 Ibid., 5.

52 Ibid., 4.

53 Nick Stratt, "Microsoft's HoloLens Explained: How it Works and Why It's Different," CNET (January 24, 1015).

54 Caetlin Benson-Allott, "Undoing Violence: Politics, Genre, and Duration in Kathryn Bigelow's Cinema," *Film Quarterly* 64, no. 2 (Winter 2010): 33.

55 Fredric Jameson, *Archaeologies of the Future: A Desire Called Utopia and Other Science Fictions* (New York and London: Verso, 2005), 384

56 William Gibson, "Talk for Book Expo, New York," *Distrust That Particular Flavor* (New York: Berkley Trade/Penguin Books, 2012), 46.

57 Another Bible in circulation in Shakespeare's time was the 1599 Geneva Bible, which translates the line quite similarly: "For now we see through a glass darkly: but then *shall we see* face to face. Now I know in part: but then shall I know even as I am known."

58 http://www.inamo-restaurant.com.

59 John Silcox, "BMW i8 Cruises into Mission Impossible Movie," *TheChargingPoint.com* (December 16, 2011).

60 In many ways, this book has significant intersections with a range of books emerging about material culture studies, which remains an important, popular, and extremely creative field of the humanities. *Glass* offers a case study for those thinking through texts such as Jonathan Lamb's *The Things Things Say* (Princeton: Princeton University Press, 2011), Ian Bogost's *Alien Phenomenology, or What It's Like to Be a Thing* (Minneapolis: University of Minnesota Press, 2012) or Levi Bryant's *The Democracy of Objects* (Ann Arbor: University of Michigan Library, 2011). Indeed, my book describes a point of view that embraces what Bryant has termed an "onticology," where "being itself is composed of objects," as well as relations between objects, rendering visible how subjects themselves are inevitably objects.

61 The encounter with Merlin's magic glass occurs in Book Three, cantos two and three. Edmund Spenser, *The Faerie Queene: Books Three and Four*, ed. Dorothy Stephens (Indianapolis and Cambridge: Hackett Publishing Company, 2006), 30–68.

62 John Dee gives us another, stunning example where the world is made of glass: "The whole frame of God's creatures, (which is the whole world,) is to us, a bright glass: from which, by reflection, rebounds to our knowledge and perseverance, beames, and radiations: representing the Image of his Infinite goodness, omnipotence, and wisdom. And we thereby, are taught and persuaded to glorify our Creator, as God: and be thankful therefore". Dee, sig. bjv.

63 "The Truly Personal Computer," *The Economist* (February 28 to March 6, 2015), 19.

64 iPhones, as well as many other smartphones and tablets, use Corning's "Gorilla Glass" for their screens. The product name, like those for other forms of interactive glass such as Iris Glass, Willow Glass, and Lotus Glass, once again invite us to see glass as connected to life.

INDEX

Page references for illustrations appear in *italics*.